WITHDRAWN
KIRTLEY LIBRARY
COLUMBIA COLLEGE
COLUMBIA, MO 65216

THE MARKET PLANNING GUIDE

A handbook to help you design, write, and use a
marketing plan
tailored to your specific business needs.

Upstart Publishing Company, Inc.
The Small Business Publishing Company
12 Portland Street
Dover, NH 03820
Telephone: 603-749-5071
Outside of NH: 1-800-235-8866

Publishers of:
The Business Planning Guide
The Personnel Planning Guide
The Market Planning Guide
The Market Planning Guide Workbook
The Cash Flow Control Guide
Common Sense Management Techniques
and other publications for small business owners

About the Author

David H. Bangs, Jr., is President of Upstart Publishing Company, Inc., which he founded in 1977. As developer of the company's product lines, he authored *The Business Planning Guide* (which has sold over 150,000 copies), *The Personnel Planning Guide*, *The Cash Flow Control Guide*, *The Market Planning Guide*, and over 30 *Common Sense Management Techniques* topics.

Prior to founding Upstart, Mr. Bangs honed his business management and communication skills. He was coordinator of the Business Information Center in Exeter, New Hampshire, a pilot project for a Federal Reserve Bank of Boston regional economic development plan. For several years, Mr. Bangs was a commercial loan officer at Bank of America in Los Angeles, where he worked with small high-tech businesses. At the University of New Hampshire, Mr. Bangs taught courses on logic and the philosophy of science.

Mr. Bangs lives in Portsmouth, New Hampshire with his wife, Lacey, and Thud, their black lab. Four of their five children are in college.

Copyright © 1987 by David H. Bangs, Jr., and Upstart Publishing Company, Inc.
All rights reserved.
Second printing.
Printed in the United States of America.

Library of Congress Catalog Number 86-051424

Reproduction of this material in whole or in part by any means without the express written consent of the publisher is expressly prohibited.

ISBN # 0-936894-16-4

Published by: Upstart Publishing Company, Inc.
                Dover, New Hampshire 03802

Table of Contents

About the Author ii
To the Reader v
Foreword vii
Introduction ix
Chapter One: Marketing Overview 1
Chapter Two: Products and Services 11
Chapter Three: Customers and Prospects 23
Chapter Four: Competitive Analysis 33
Chapter Five: Price, Location, and Sales Practices 41
Chapter Six: Strengths and Weaknesses 53
Chapter Seven: Advertising and Promotion 63
Chapter Eight: Strategic Marketing 79
Chapter Nine: The Marketing Plan 89
Chapter Ten: The Sales Plan 93
Appendix One: Summary of Questions and Marketing Plan Outline 99
Appendix Two: Bibliography and Resources 103

To the Reader

Upstart Publishing Company's mission is to provide useful, applicable, proven management tools to small business owners everywhere. As a former banker and as an entrepreneur, I've learned (sometimes painfully) what the roadblocks to small business success are, and how to overcome or avoid them.

That's where our products come into play.

The Business Planning Guide came first. It is used by hundreds of banks, schools, and organizations which help small business owners take control of their businesses, as well as by thousands and thousands of individuals. The book guides readers through the strategic process of deciding what the company will be, based on the reader's resources and competitive and economic positions.

Common Sense became the next item in our tool kit. *The Business Planning Guide* generated a lot of questions: How do I find and retain good employees? How can I sell my products or services? How can I meet payroll when sales slack off? We packaged our answers in a monthly newsletter format, and have syndicated it to banks (ranging in size from Chase Manhattan to Granite State National) and other organizations with small business interests (General Business Services, Goodyear Tire and Rubber Company, National Association of Women Business Owners, to name a few). This extensive and ongoing small business reader base has provided a lot of suggestions and ideas.

This information flow has led us Upstarts (my colleagues and me) to think of small businesses as composed of four important systems: business planning, personnel, marketing, and financing. If these systems are covered adequately, the small business will succeed. If one or more of the systems is ignored or seriously flawed, the business will fail.

The Business Planning Guide addresses the widest range of problems, and as a result, covers just the tips of the icebergs of personnel, marketing, and finance. *The Personnel Planning Guide* and *The Market Planning Guide* were written to remedy this limitation. If a small business owner has a clear business plan, good employees, and an action-oriented marketing plan, the financing will follow. (The business plan itself is a kind of financing proposal, and will help pinpoint capital and financing needs.)

Cash flow—the actual movement of money in and out of a going business—is more complicated. Our *Cash Flow Control Guide* has been designed to help small business owners manage their cash flow more effectively, and to rely less on debt.

We know the techniques and methods described in these books and the more than 60 *Common Sense* topics work. They have worked for Upstart. They have worked for hundreds of thousands of small business owners all over the U.S. and all over the world. They aren't fancy. They don't call for advanced business degrees.

They do require you to put them to work. Apply them, and take control of your business. We can provide the tools, but you have to use them.

Special thanks are in order for Andrea Axman, Upstart's Senior Editor, who has spent hundreds of hours revising and improving *The Market Planning Guide* and interviewing small business owners, as well as performing her editorial tasks. She does this for all of our books, as well as for the very customized publications we write for some of our banking clients. I hope I can be as helpful to her in her forthcoming book, *Personal Financial Planning Guide*, as she has been to me and to Upstart's other writers.

David H. Bangs, Jr.
Portsmouth, New Hampshire
October 1988

Foreword

Entrepreneurial enthusiasm is both an asset and a liability.

All too often, the entrepreneurial enthusiasm which gives birth to a company and drives it through its earliest successes contributes to the firm's eventual demise. Often, this is due to the entrepreneur's preoccupation with "product" and "process." In the quest for producing a new and better product or service, the entrepreneur tends to overlook whether or not a market actually exists for the product—or whether the product can be brought to market in a profitable way.

The Market Planning Guide is valuable because it can help entrepreneurs avoid expensive mistakes—and the pain that results from those mistakes. This book painlessly guides the entrepreneur through the process of a) identifying the product, b) analyzing the firm's market and competitive position, and c) focusing upon the firm's strengths. *The Market Planning Guide* succeeds because it presents sophisticated marketing theory in a non-threatening, interactive way.

The Market Planning Guide is based on a series of questions which even the most product-oriented entrepreneur will be able to answer. In answering these questions—and learning why they were asked—the entrepreneur will be exposed and sensitized to a new way of looking at products and services, markets, and the competition. After reading *The Market Planning Guide*, the entrepreneur will be less concerned with the specifics of producing a particular widget or service and more concerned with questions like:
- Do widget buyers actually exist?
- Do we have a product which satisfies their needs?
- Do we have the resources necessary to reach widget buyers?
- Who else is making widgets?
- How does our widget differ from theirs?
- Why should people buy our widgets instead of theirs?

In answering these questions, entrepreneurs will not only gain a firmer understanding of the tasks which lie ahead in advertising and promoting their product or service, they'll be preparing a comprehensive marketing plan which managers of any Fortune 500 division would be proud to present to their stockholders and senior management.

The most important books are those which cause long-lasting changes in attitude. Unfortunately, few marketing books are able to fundamentally change the typical entrepreneur's basic preoccupation with product and process. This is because most marketing texts are so theoretical that entrepreneurs have difficulty relating them to their daily duties. *The Market Planning Guide*, however, succeeds because it is based entirely on defining and meeting particular marketing challenges. This increases the reader's involvement and helps the book drive home its lessons in the most powerful way possible.

Working through the steps outlined in this book can contribute to entrepreneurial success—as well as prevent unnecessary hardships and financial loss. *The Market Planning Guide* should be "required reading" for new entrepreneurs and "recommended reading" for seasoned entrepreneurs, who may have forgotten some of the basics necessary for continued business success.

Roger C. Parker,
Marketing Consultant
Seattle, Washington
February 20, 1987

Introduction

"What needs improving at your business? Marketing and sales capability was the response given most by nearly 1,300 executives—70% of them at small firms—who responded to a poll by the CPA firm of Ernst & Whinney...."
The Wall Street Journal; February 6, 1984; page 27.

A marketing plan is a detailed, written plan that lays out the steps your company must take to create customers, thereby achieving its sales and marketing objectives.

Good marketing calls for performing many small tasks thoroughly and intelligently. It also requires that you have good products/services, and that you know your customers and prospects better than your competitors do.

Once you analyze your products/services, customers, and prospects, and understand what your competitors are up to, you can develop effective strategies to achieve your sales and marketing goals. Most small business owners don't bother to take these extra steps, preferring to plunge ahead and either copy someone or take unnecessary chances. This might be called the "Man of Action" problem, since so many small business owners pride themselves on being doers instead of thinkers. Actually, you have to be both to succeed in business. First, you need a plan, so that your marketing efforts are not random decisions. Then, you have to act to make your plans work.

We worked with a small accounting firm, R.C. Montville and Company, CPAs, to create the marketing plan used as the example in the text of *The Market Planning Guide*. Accounting firms have especially acute marketing problems, since they sell intangible services. What's more, accounting services are almost impossible to differentiate. Accounting reports (tax, financial, management information) all look more or less alike. But the principles of marketing apply in all businesses. What are you selling? Who buys from you? Is the business profitable—or can it become profitable? How do you let people know what you have for sale? Why should they buy from you?

R.C. Montville and Company have set their goals and established the action steps needed to reach those goals. By following their reasoning—and filling in the blank forms provided in *The Market Planning Guide Workbook*, using Montville as a model—you can create an effective marketing plan suited to your goals and resources. *(The Market Planning Guide Workbook* is available from Upstart Publishing Company, Inc., 12 Portland Street, Dover, NH 03820, or by calling 749-5071 in New Hampshire, or (800) 235-8866 from out of state.)

This will create a significant marketing edge for you. It doesn't matter what your business is. You can own a shoe store, or a grocery, or a restaurant, or a job shop, or a medical practice. It doesn't matter. Your competitors probably don't organize their businesses on marketing principles. In effect, they create customers for you to profit from. All you have to do is follow the steps outlined in this book, develop strategies for your business, and then implement those strategies. This isn't easy—but it winds up being a lot easier than proceeding without a clear marketing plan.

And a lot more profitable.

Whatever you do, don't fall into the trap of looking at marketing as a luxury that you can cut at the first sign of a sales slump. Marketing is an investment in the future of your business. No matter how good your product or service may be, or how terrific a location you have, you will still have to practice careful marketing. Slow sales and slumping profits are marketing problems. Loss of market share is a marketing problem.

If you want to increase your sales, profits, and market share, then increase and improve your marketing efforts. Hire an expert if you can't do it yourself. But don't do what too many small business owners do: Do not stop marketing efforts because "you can't afford marketing." That's a false economy of the worst kind. It will put you out of business.

Chapter One:
Marketing Overview

The sole purpose of your business is to create customers.

Technological excellence, delivery capability, service skills, pricing theory, and product perfection will, at best, gain you nothing if you can't create customers.

"Marketing" is the complex process of creating customers for your products/services. A marketing plan is a written document which helps you manage this process—including the action steps needed to make the plan work.

Your marketing plan calls for thoughtful answers to 30 major questions. These questions are highlighted throughout the text of *The Market Planning Guide*. A complete list of these major questions is provided in Appendix One.

Writing the plan is easy. You don't write the plan itself until you've done 95% of the work. The tough part of market planning is a careful analysis of:
1. Your product/service;
2. Your markets and your position in those markets; and
3. Your business' strengths and weaknesses.

Planning cannot be done in a vacuum. The first step is to take a broad overview of your marketing efforts (including your current markets and your products/services) in the context of current economic and competitive conditions.

Begin by answering the following questions. Don't aim for 100% accuracy. You can fine tune your answers later.

Question 1: What business are you in?
If you have written a business plan, you have already gone through this exercise. If not, ask:
- *What are your products/services?* Your business definition is based on what you sell.
- *Who are your customers?* Your present customer base and the target markets you want to serve help focus the definition further.
- *Why do your customers buy from you?* There are plenty of competitors for every business, and a wide range of other products and services for your customers and prospects to buy.
- *What sets your business apart from your competitors'?* What's distinct or unusual about your business? If you can differentiate yourself from your competitors in the eyes of your market, you gain a strong advantage.

Your definition of your business will determine the direction your business takes. If you can state clearly and succinctly what you sell, to whom, and why they buy from you, you are well on the way to creating an effective marketing plan.

> **The sole purpose of your business is to create customers.**

If you can state clearly and succinctly what you sell, to whom, and why they buy from you, you are well on the way to creating an effective marketing plan.

Imagine yourself traveling in an airplane. You strike up a conversation with the person sitting next to you, who asks, "What business are you in?" How would you answer? Your response should be brief, but clear and specific.

There is no "right" answer. A series of answers evolves as your business changes. Your products/services and markets change. So does your competitive position. Other people will copy what you do well, and compete for your customers on price, quality, service, or wherever you appear vulnerable.

All your market planning efforts are an attempt to elaborate on your answer to that seemingly simple question, "What business are you in?"

Question 2: What do you sell?
What are you selling? Computers? Landscape designs? Real estate? Clothing? Legal advice? Fish? Medical services? Baseball bats?

In Chapter Two you will return to your product/service list from a different angle. For now, just list the products/services you sell in Figure 1.2 in your *Market Planning Guide Workbook*.

Question 3: What are your target markets?
Target marketing is a simple concept. You have a limited number of marketing dollars. Your business has a potential market consisting of a vaguely defined group of people who might buy your products. In order to invest your money wisely you have to narrow that broad group down to those persons (or persons in particular institutions) most likely to buy from you.

Many potential buyers are too far away geographically, can't afford your prices, don't want to change suppliers, prefer to deal locally, or are unlikely for other reasons to become your customers. Recognizing these limitations on your market is the first step toward target marketing. Next, identify the segments of the overall market which are most likely to buy from you. (See Chapter Three, pages 24 through 27 for more on this.)

What is target marketing? Look at Figure 1.1. The bull's eye is worth $10 in sales, the first ring $5, the next ring $3, the final ring $1. Missing the target is a dead loss.

Now suppose you need $100 in sales to break even, and you have a marketing budget of $15 (for the sake of the illustration, think of that as 15 arrows). In order to meet your $100 goal, you need at least five bull's eyes. Any fewer and you can't achieve your goal of $100. Needless to say, you'd take considerable care with each arrow.

To push the simile a bit further, you'd find that your marksmanship improves with practice, that taking careful note of surrounding conditions is important, and that focusing on your target pays off. Shooting at one random target after another is harder, and makes your expensively gathered experience useless. So does changing your bow, or forgetting to keep score.

In marketing, you have to keep track of what you're up to. Fashions change. The economic climate changes. Products and services gain and lose value. Markets shift. But you will always have a finite number of arrows (marketing dollars), and you will always find that once you have the range on a target it pays off to keep shooting at that target until you have good reasons to shoot at a new one.

Figure 1.1
Target Marketing

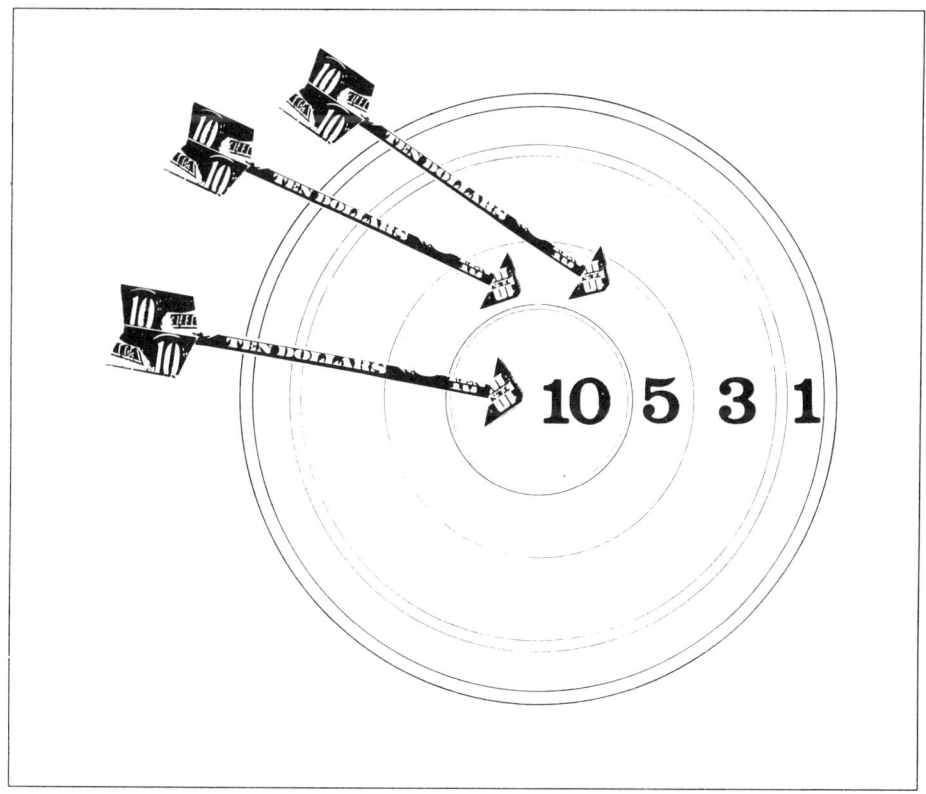

Target marketing is an ongoing process. You want to know:
1. What are your products and services? You've made a first cut at this one.
2. Who is most likely to buy them from you?
3. What characteristics (wants, needs, habits, and so forth) do your customers and hottest prospects share? Segment or differentiate the market.
4. How big are your marketing segments?
5. What is the most profitable segment mix, in terms of ease and cost of sales, sales volume, and price? Rank the segments in terms of potential profitability for your business.

For each product/service, what are the target markets? Jot them down on Figure 1.2 in your *Market Planning Guide Workbook*.

Figure 1.2
Product/Service and Market List

If you have many products/services, try to bundle them together into no more than 10 categories. You can always expand the list later—but for now, keep it simple.

Product/Service	Target Markets
1. Business consulting	Manufacturers, service firms and retailers with sales of $700,000 to $5,000,000
2. Monthly accounting services	
3. Audits	
4. Tax return preparation	
5. Tax consultation & representation	
6. Special projects	
7. Other accounting services	
8.	
9.	
10.	

Question 4: What are your marketing goals for next year? Your sales and profit goals?

You need two sets of goals: for your business and for yourself. Your personal goals come first. You want to be sure you don't commit your business to a strategy which runs counter to your personal wishes. Do you want to sell your business in a few years and retire? Build the business to Fortune 1,000 size, or keep it small? Be a technological trailblazer? All of these have been cited by small business owners, and each has profound marketing implications.

Figure 1.3
Your Personal Goals

1. How much money do you want, or need, to earn? $60,000

2. What sort of lifestyle is desirable for you and your family? Affluent

3. How big do you want your business to be? Sales of $250,000

4. How will your business reflect you and your values? I want to be fair to my employees and to my clients.

5. What are your risk parameters? What is your tolerance for risk? Ours is not a business to take risks — we need achievable goals.

6. What do you want to achieve in five years? Semi-retirement

Some plausible marketing goals for the immediate future are increased dollar or unit sales, improved market share, greater profits, entry into new markets, abandoning a current market, and adopting a new technology or product line. Maybe you want to improve your company's image, advertising, or promotional efforts. Or implement a new pricing strategy or distribution process.

You need two sets of goals for your business. Your personal goals come first.

Be general. These goals will be reexamined and refocused. To turn these vague goals into real objectives, you have to do more. Objectives involve specific numbers and time frames. For now, you will jot down the broad marketing goals you would like to achieve over the next year and over the next three years in Figure 1.5 of your *Market Planning Guide Workbook*.

Sales and profit goals can be more precise.

If you have a small number of product/service lines, break the goals down further. But even an aggregate number is helpful; you can break it down later. For each product/service and target market of Figure 1.2, forecast sales for the next year in Figure 1.4. A worst case/best case/most likely case approach makes this somewhat easier and more accurate than just guessing. A product-by-product approach produces a more accurate forecast than lumping all your sales together in one undifferentiated heap.

Figure 1.4
Sales Approach

For each product/service or product line, estimate what sales would be if everything goes wrong next year. Then estimate what sales would be if everything goes perfectly. Since neither case is likely, an in-between sales figure will be a more accurate forecast.

Sales Forecast

Product/Service	Worst Case	Most Likely Case	Best Case
1. Business Consulting	$25,000	$30,000	$40,000
2. Monthly Accounting Services	$25,000	$30,000	$40,000
3. Audits	$10,000	$20,000	$30,000
4. Tax Return Preparation	$25,000	$30,000	$30,000
5. Tax Consultation & Representation	$20,000	$25,000	$30,000
6. Special Projects	$15,000	$20,000	$30,000
7. Other Accounting Services	$15,000	$20,000	$25,000
8.			
9.			
10.			
TOTAL:	$135,000	$175,000	$225,000

Profit goals are harder to establish. If you know what profit you traditionally make as a percentage of sales, use the sales forecast and add a bit. You don't want to set goals too low, and you will (you hope) become more profitable with more sales. Experience and time will correct or corroborate your hopes.

Note that Figure 1.5 gives you both a dollar figure and a time frame. This makes your broad objectives more precise, which helps you set up benchmarks to test progress and measure improvement.

Figure 1.5
Preliminary Marketing, Sales, and Profit Goals

Marketing Goals:
1. *Develop a program for small business financial management*
2. *Develop a program for more management consulting and less accounting*
3.
4.
5.

Sales Goals for Each Product/Service (see Figure 1.4 for next year's most likely figures):

	For Next Year	In Three Years
1. *Business consulting*	$30,000	$45,000
2. *Monthly accounting*	$30,000	$45,000
3. *Audits*	$20,000	$40,000
4. *Tax return preparation*	$30,000	$35,000
5. *Tax consultation & representation*	$25,000	$35,000
6. *Special projects*	$20,000	$35,000
7. *Other accounting services*	$20,000	$30,000
Profit Goals:	$175,000	$265,000
	$50,000 profit	*at least $100,000*

Comments:

Question 5: What might keep you from achieving these goals?
Possible barriers include cash flow problems or capital shortages, personnel deficiencies or inefficiencies, weak technology, stale product lines, pricing woes, declining or flat sales, strong new competitors, quality control problems, and many more.

Every company has limitations. A smart small business owner or manager knows what the problems are and addresses them. The ostrich-like manager, on the other hand, is always receiving nasty blind-side surprises.

Some problems are long-term: A job shop printer has to be concerned about laser printing, not because the technology is widespread but because it will be, and it will change his or her business. Being a supplier to a declining industry is a long-term problem. So is being located in a stagnant or declining local economy.

Product and service limitations might involve quality control, rejected raw inventories, stock-outs, delivery problems, lack of skilled service personnel, or old equipment that puts you at a time and cost disadvantage.

Know your limitations. Then correct them—or adjust your marketing plans to accommodate them. Follow Figure 1.6 and keep a list of problems that you think might get between you and your goals. The finest memory is not so firm as faded ink. Write them down in your *Market Planning Guide Workbook*.

A smart small business owner or manager knows what the problems are and addresses them.

Figure 1.6
Obstacles We Could Face

Today's Date: *4/5/81*

What problems am I avoiding?
1. *Cash flow: slow paying clients and collections are difficult*
2. *Educational updates: necessary but difficult to produce*
3. *Setting clear, consistent fees*

What problems might prevent us from reaching our marketing, sales, and profit goals?
1. *Time* — *We have a vicious circle!*
2. *Being understaffed* — *Once our cash flow is up,*
3. _____ *then we can deal with*
4. _____ *these problems.*
5. _____

What are we going to do about these problems?
1. Assign responsibility to individuals to achieve solutions.
2. Allocate resources and authority to these people.
3. Establish benchmarks and deadlines to help them monitor their progress.

We want to increase our cash flow in 3 months, and we want to add personnel in 6 months.

> **Marketing is as much a cost of doing business as rent or payroll.**

Note that Figure 1.6 calls for action. A marketing plan has to be implemented, or it's a waste of time. Dramatic changes in your business will come from correcting errors and problems. More lasting and profitable, if less splashy, changes result from implementing a carefully thought-out marketing strategy.

Question 6: What is your marketing budget?
This is a trick question. If you have a marketing budget, you can answer it. If you don't, you have the most common problem: no budget at all. The second most common small business budgeting problem is relying on a reactive, sloppy, "whatever is available if I have no better use for it" excuse for a budget.

Marketing is as much a cost of doing business as rent or payroll. It isn't a "cost center" to cut at the first sign of a sales slump or reduce to boost profits for a month or two. If you don't have a marketing budget, or if you think your current budget needs improvement, go no further. You have to have a budget— unless you want to waste money and forego sales and profit improvement.

Anyone can set a budget. Setting a budget worth following requires a lot of skill.

One more common method of setting a marketing budget is to allocate a fixed percentage of forecast sales on a calendar basis. You can get trade figures. Ask your business counselor, accountant, banker, or other financial experts such as editors of trade magazines. Ask other successful business owners. These figures will provide some useful guidelines.

Just remember that more than advertising and public relations come out of your marketing budget. What do sales cost you? Sales training? Preparation of window displays? Sales support and presentation pieces? Check out Figure 1.7. Your marketing budget has to reflect your business, not someone else's.

Look at your marketing, sales, and profit goals in Figure 1.5. Try to figure out what it will cost to reach them. If it is more than you can afford, fine. That forces some choices upon you. You need a marketing budget you can live with, one that helps you reach your goals and doesn't tie you to a formula that can't adjust to sudden shifts.

The best marketing budgets have two parts: first, a fixed, monthly amount to meet ongoing, monthly marketing expenses; second, a contingency or project budget to help you meet unexpected marketing needs. A new market may open up, a competitor may retire, or new competition may appear. How you respond to these opportunities and challenges is heavily influenced by your budget.

You know your marketing, sales, and profit goals. Discuss these with your accountant or business advisors. Marketing without money is like making bricks without straw. It can't be done without divine intervention—and that kind of marketing help cannot be relied on.

Figure 1.7
Marketing Budget Items

This is not an exhaustive list. Use it as a starting point. Your company will use some of these categories plus others peculiar to your marketing needs.

1. Selling (direct costs)
   Sales salaries and commissions $ _____
   Travel $ *1,000*
   Entertainment $ *2,000*
2. Selling (indirect costs)
   Training $ _____
   Marketing research $ _____
   Statistical analysis $ _____
   Subscriptions and dues $ *5,000*
3. Advertising $ *2,000*
4. Sales promotion other than advertising $ *10,000*
5. Public relations $ *500*
6. Shipping and handling
   Order filling, packaging $ _____
   Postage and cartage $ *1,800*
7. Credits and collection
   Administrative expense $ _____
   Bad-debt allowance $ _____
8. Marketing administration $ _____

Incomplete campaigns eat profits, so make sure you have enough money to finish your marketing campaigns.

To set up your budgets, use your resources. Your accountant or financial advisors can help you put dollar costs to your goals more efficiently than you can. However, you can provide estimates based on your goals and prior experience in your business. Sketch in your first rough estimates in Figure 1.8.

Figure 1.8
Preliminary Marketing Budget Estimates

Made by: *GL*   Date: *2/5/87*
Reviewed by: _____ Date: _____

Goal or Action: (e.g., Advertising)	Timing: monthly	Costs: $750/month)
Yellow Page ad	annually	$100/month
Chamber of Commerce	2 ads/year	$50/ad
Brochure		$2000/year
Brochure mailing	4 times/year	$800/year
Misc. ads	2 times/year	$400/year

Total: $ *4,500/year*

Use this for rough estimates only. You need your accountant's help in setting up your final marketing budget.

Summary for Chapter One
1. Preliminary goals (personal, marketing, sales, profit) have been established for the next year and the next three years. (See Figures 1.3 and 1.5.)
2. Some problems have been identified and initial corrective steps taken. (See Figure 1.6.)
3. Your products and services have been listed in Figure 1.2.
4. Your target markets have been identified and linked with your products/services in Figure 1.2.
5. A marketing budget estimate has been made in Figure 1.8.

In your *Market Planning Guide Workbook*, fill in Figures 1.2, 1.3, 1.5, 1.6, and 1.8 to refer to in subsequent chapters. Your marketing plan will grow from these initial assumptions and estimates.

A list of effective small business marketing strategies is given in Chapter Eight. (See Figure 8.4 on page 84.) As you work through the planning process, your strategic choices will begin to emerge.

Chapter Two:
Products and Services

If you are already in business, you already have products/services, markets, and problems. If you are about to begin a business, you probably have a clear idea of what, where, when, and to whom you will be selling.

The leading theoretical approach to marketing demands that you first determine what your markets want, then provide a way to satisfy them profitably. That's fine if you have the luxury of choosing your target market and product/service mix. Most of us, though, are limited by our experience and interests, to say nothing of other limitations such as money, family obligations, and so forth.

What can you do if you are already in business? Make haste slowly. Change gradually to a marketing orientation. Understand your target markets in depth, and measure the products/services you offer against the demands of those markets. You can change product and service lines over time to meet the changing demands of your customers and prospects. But you can't suddenly switch—it takes planning and time.

There are powerful constraints on the kinds of products and services you can offer: money, time, customer habits, competition, and technology are a few. Creating demand for a new product and changing consumer buying habits is close to impossible. Introducing a new technology can bankrupt you. The number of truly innovative products or services introduced each year is tiny, and beyond the scope of this book.

Most products and services offered by small businesses are generic. While you may think that your products and services are special, that perception is not necessarily shared by your market.

To gain a competitive advantage, do two things:
1. Know your products/services better than the competition knows theirs.
2. Know the benefits of your products/services from your customers' perspective.

Understand the benefits your customers can get from your products or services. Look at your business from their point of view: Without a strong reason to think otherwise, one hardware store is like another; lawyers are interchangeable; seafood markets are where you buy fish. What's so special about your screwdrivers, or your wills, or your halibut?

People buy benefits. What they want is not necessarily what you think you are selling. They buy solutions to their problems. They buy satisfaction of needs and wants. The solutions and satisfactions are the benefits they buy along with your products/services.

People buy solutions to their problems and satisfaction for their wants and needs.

The more reasons to buy you can communicate to your target markets the better.

Question 7: What are the benefits of your products/services?
A careful product/service line analysis goes beyond a list of what you currently sell, and far beyond product knowledge. Not that these are unimportant pieces of information—in fact, that's where product/service line analysis begins.

1. *List the products/services you currently sell.* (Go back and refer to Figure 1.2.) You may want to reorganize or recategorize them, or add to your list. Enter the products or services on Figure 2.4.

Before you can match up products/services and markets, you have to form a clear idea of what needs and wants those products and services satisfy. Any product or service can satisfy a number of wants and needs. While people don't always know why they buy what they buy, you can draw some useful conclusions by observing and inquiring.

Think of several applications for each product or service, and several sets of wants and needs they satisfy. By communicating this to your target markets, you greatly increase the market appeal of those products and services. The more reasons to buy you can communicate to your target markets the better.

2. *For each product or service, ask: What is its purpose?* What needs or wants does it satisfy for your customers? For your prospects? Jot down the most obvious needs and wants each product or service satisfies on Figure 2.4. This will give you a better understanding of the markets you can reasonably target and provide the underpinnings of your marketing strategy.

What kinds of wants and needs should you consider in Figure 2.4? Marketing gurus have listed thousands. A handful are offered in Figure 2.1.

3. *For each product or service, ask: Is it a breadwinner now, or will it be in the future? Is it past its prime? Should it be continued? Or given more support (financial, personnel, promotion)?* You want to put your resources to work where they'll have the best long-term payoff.

4. *Should you expand your current product/service lines?* Sometimes sales of one product reveal customer needs for another. If a significant number of your customers ask for a product that would be an extension of your current lines, the risk of extending your product lines may be worth taking. It takes less effort to cross-sell to your old customers than it does to create new customers.

Ask product-line questions quarterly. We get so attached to the old product line that we forget to update it. Meanwhile the market moves away.

5. *What are the particular advantages/disadvantages of each product or service as compared with competitive products and services?* Product/service comparisons tip you off to competitive positioning. In chapter four, "Competitive Analysis," further marketing comparisons will help keep you ahead of the competition. For now, take special note of differences in target markets and benefits advertised.

Figure 2.1
Why Do People Buy Things?

Even though individuals ultimately make all purchasing decisions, their approaches will differ depending on whether they are buying for themselves or buying for their company or institution. Several ways of looking at buyer wants and needs are shown here.

Basis for wanting things:
1. To fill biological needs
2. To gain security
3. To get status
4. To gain recognition
5. To satisfy aggressions
6. To satisfy sensibilities
7. To lessen anxiety
8. To save time

Some buyer motivations:
1. Satisfaction of the senses
2. Imitation of other people
3. Stylishness
4. Profit
5. Convenience
6. Knowledge
7. Comfort
8. Fear
9. Pride
10. Curiosity
11. Pleasure
12. Self expression or self-actualization
13. Gaining an advantage
14. Saving money

For institutional markets, important motivations to buy include:
1. Dependability
2. Discounts for bulk orders
3. Price and quality
4. Relationship with current vendors
5. Customization
6. Market exclusivity
7. Value
8. Delivery schedules
9. Guarantees
10. Safety for the purchasing agent ("You don't get in trouble buying IBM..." attitude is a good example of bureaucratic thinking. The IBM choice isn't necessarily the best, but it's viewed as defensible.)

Figure 2.2
Product Comparison Form

Fill this out for each product or service you offer. For the sake of simplicity, compare yours only to the leading competitive products or services.

Product/Service: _All of our accounting services_

	Yours:	The Competition's:
Target markets:	Mfg, service and retail co's w/ sales of $700,000 to $3,000,000	Large corporations & their executives; some small businesses
Benefits offered:		
1.	Aggressive sales approach	Passive sales approach
2.	Timely service	→
3.	Use of computers	→
Quality	Very good	→
Price	On the low side	Higher fees
Improved versions		
Location	Convenient — will visit client when necessary	→
Delivery	Meet client's deadlines	→
Follow-up service	Excellent	Good
Availability	Very good	Good
Convenience		
Reliability	Good	→
Service	Excellent	Depends how big account is
Guarantees	No satisfaction, no charge	?
Other (specify):		
1.	Experience with small business owners	Not as much experience with this market
2.	Active approach to solving clients' problems	Defensive approach
3.		

14

Comparisons are another place you may discover new applications, new product ideas, and new opportunities. Look outside your business. Maybe the competition has a wider line, or a more specialized line. Would this make sense for your business? Maybe their packaging is better, or their distribution or delivery system is superior. Perhaps their advertising is stronger. Adapt Figure 2.2 to compare product mix, product lines, or other areas where you might be able to gain a competitive edge.

6. *Have you made improvements in your products or services lately? Are you planning any?* You don't want your products and services to become stale or old hat, or be made obsolete by your competitors' changes. This is more than a question of style or fads. "New! Improved!" is a great marketing line, especially if the product or service is really new and improved. Improvements are a powerful positioning tool: Who doesn't want the improved model?

7. *What new products and services are you planning?* Should you develop new ones? Fill out a product line? Meet competition? Or should you prune back your product line to the most profitable elements?

One of the most powerful marketing strategies for small businesses is to locate and dominate market niches too small or too specialized for bigger companies to profitably invade. Quite often this calls for new products or highly specialized sets of skills. However, any new product or service cries out for strong marketing justification. Otherwise, it's all too easy to squander your resources on exciting but unprofitable new ventures.

8. *What are possible substitutes for your goods or services?* Are there any new developments (technological, social, economic) that might result in new ways of satisfying your market's wants and needs?

Not all dangers and opportunities are obvious. The only way to keep abreast of what might affect your business is to read, attend trade or other business shows, and keep your eyes and ears open. Your chances of picking up on an opportunity are far greater than your competitors' if you periodically review and analyze your product and service lines.

9. *Can you list at least five new applications for your products/services?* Repackaged products or new applications of old products open up new marketing opportunities. For the product grid (Figure 2.7), think of new applications as new products.

Huge marketing gains have come from new applications of old products and services. You can sometimes repackage or reposition a product or service to appeal to a wider market, or to deepen penetration of your current markets. A classic example of repackaging is Arm and Hammer baking soda. It sells more widely as a refrigerator cleaner and air freshener than it ever did as a baking soda.

Ask questions. Ask your customers, suppliers, sales force, and other interested persons what your products and services might be used for. Their answers might provide new applications that result in tomorrow's sales.

Target market and benefit differences are important pieces of information for your marketing plans.

Your aim is to develop an image of offering something special.

Use the answers and ideas you generate to fill out Figure 2.3 in your *Market Planning Guide Workbook* for each product or service.

Figure 2.3
Product/Service Application Worksheet

Product/Service: *Accounting and management advisory services.*

What are its features? *Preparing tax returns & financial statements. analyzing cash flow and balance sheets; making recommendations.*

What benefits does it produce? *Helps business owner save money and use his/her financial resources better.*

How is it used? *When client needs help solving problems.*

How is it purchased (unit, bulk, with other products)? Which other products? *With other services, usually a result of doing client's tax return.*

What are other possible applications of this product/service? *Could apply to personal financial planning for business owners — we could offer appropriate services.*

Use these ideas to rethink how your products might be marketed. As an example, basketballs are used as float valves in some industrial applications. Their features of toughness, uniform size and quality, roundness, and buoyancy make them ideal for this purpose.

Now put the two concepts together: What wants and needs do your products fill? Who might have these wants and needs?

Question 8: What is special about your products/services?
What is the "unique selling proposition" for your product and service lines? For each product and service? Is it quality? Price? Convenience? Style? Professionalism? What sets your products and services apart from the rest? The information gathered in Figure 2.2 helps you determine the unique selling proposition of your products.

Your aim is to develop an image of offering something special. Your neighborhood convenience store has a unique selling proposition: You can get a loaf of bread or a jar of mayonnaise at any time without getting in your car. Look at competing businesses and ask what's special about them. Can those insights help you position and define your business? Every business has something special to recommend it. What's your claim?

You may want to stress quality, or dominate your market through price competition.

Figure 2.4
Product/Service Benefits and Markets

Your Product/Service	Benefits It Offers (Wants/Needs Fulfilled)	Possible Target Markets
1. Business consulting	Solves business owner's problems	Retail, manufacturing and service firms with sales of $700,000 to $5,000,000
2. Monthly accounting	Keeps books up-to-date	
3. Audits	Keeps clients from worrying; saves $$	
4. Tax return preparation	Tax return is done correctly	
5. Tax consultation & representation	Keeps clients from worrying; saves $$	
6. Special projects	Fulfills that client's specific need	
7. Other accounting services	Client can have whatever is needed	
8.		
9.		
10.		

Some ways to set your products apart from the competition:

1. *New, improved.* Matthew's Teak Cleaner took a messy, dangerous, splattery process and simplified it. Lotus took spreadsheets for microcomputers a step further than the competition and dominated the market for business software.

2. *Packaging.* Think that L'Eggs' profit comes from a superior stocking? Think again.

3. *Pricing.* BIC grabbed the ballpoint pen market with their 19-cent pen. On the other hand, lack of courage in pricing is a major weakness for small business. A Cadillac costs only $500 more to manufacture than a Pontiac; the price differential is thousands of dollars. Price and image march together.

4. *Advertising* and *promotion.* What really is the difference between McDonald's and Burger King? Or think of Frank Perdue and his chickens. Chicken is chicken is chicken, or was until Frank Perdue changed our perceptions of a commodity and differentiated his product from everyone else's. You pay more for a Perdue chicken, too.

5. *Delivery*. Retail stores all over the world are being hurt by direct marketing. It's the fastest growing retail segment. Land's End, L.L. Bean, Frederick's of Hollywood, and hundreds of other merchants let you shop at home, and will quickly deliver their products to your door.

6. *Convenience*. Look at direct marketing again. Or check out your local Seven-Eleven Store. Many banks are now open for more convenient hours due to the press of competition. A bank that opens Saturday morning has a big advantage over a bank that doesn't.

7. *Follow-up service*. After-sale efforts are strong product/service differentiators. Wherever you live, Sears will service your washing machine. Today. That's a deliberate policy—and sharply contrasts with discount stores. Both after-sale service and price chopping are valid marketing strategies. But Sears makes more money in the long run by stressing service, not price. A medical practice that routinely involves its patients in their own health care by sending reminders will lose fewer customers than one that saves money by not keeping in touch.

Question 9: What product/service is the best contributor to your overhead and profits (O & P)? What product/service is the biggest drain on your overhead and profits?

This is a simple accounting question. If you can not tell quickly which product/service you sell makes the most money (net of all expenses, including marketing and sales costs, bad debts, and so forth), then you better have a talk with your accountant. This is important information with direct marketing implications: Where do you make money? Where do you lose money? How can you do more of the former and less of the latter—i.e., can you ride your strong products more? Cull the losers? Who buys the good products? Who buys the "bad" ones?

Figure 2.5
Winners and Losers

Products/services with major impact on O & P:

Contributors: Amounts:
1. *Business consulting* $ *30,000*
2. *Monthly accounting services*   *30,000*
3. *Audits*   *20,000*
4. *Tax consultation & representation*   *25,000*
5. *Special projects*   *20,000*

Detractors: Amounts:
1. *Individuals' tax returns* $ *9,000*
2. _____   _____
3. _____   _____
4. _____   _____
5. _____   _____

Label your products and services as cash cows, dogs, rising stars, and owner's ego. Cash cows are products that give you a good profit for very little effort. Dogs are money losers. Rising stars are tomorrow's cash cows. And owner's ego products or services are tomorrow's dogs, unless they fit in with wider company objectives.

Know what your products and services contribute to or take away from your business.

For now, keep it simple. What products and services make money for you? What products or services don't?

There may be excellent reasons to lose money for a while: gaining market share, acquiring mastery of a new technology or learning new skills, building today for tomorrow's profit. So a current loser is not necessarily either a dog or owner's ego. Nor is a current winner necessarily good. You may be missing out on tomorrow's markets by sticking with a product too long.

The important point: Know what your products and services contribute or take away from your business.

Figure 2.6
Product/Service Matrix

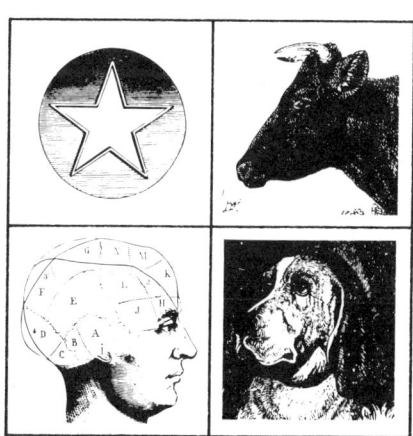

The last piece of the product/service puzzle is to look at the Product/Service Grid, Figure 2.7. Where do your leading products and services fall on this grid? Your aim is to increase sales and profits. There are four basic ways to do this.

Figure 2.7
Product/Service Grid

	Core Markets	New Target Markets
P	Old product/service	Old product/service
R	old customers	new customers
O	(lowest risk)	(risky)
D		
U	New product/service	New product/service
C	old customers	new customers
T	(risky)	(riskiest)

19

Selling new products to new customers is as risky as starting a new business.

Ask yourself how you could sell old products to new customers, or new products to old customers, before even considering selling new products to new customers. Increasing sales of old products to old customers is normally the safest way to increase sales, but may not provide a sufficiently large gain. Selling new products to new customers is as risky as starting a new business—perhaps riskier, because it can sap your energy at the expense of your current business.

All of this leads to Figure 2.8: New Product/Service Objectives. If you decide to make product or service changes, or want to provide new goodies for your target markets to purchase, treat these changes as seriously as any other major change in your business. Set objectives, including costs, deadlines, and responsibility. Implement changes carefully and systematically. Don't leave them to chance.

Use all the information gathered so far to flesh out the form. Consider improved or changed products and services to be new products or services.

Figure 2.8
New Product/Service Objectives

Person responsible: *RCM*　　　　　Review date: *2/8/87*
Product/service idea: *Business management consulting*

Benefits it will offer: *Increased profits, financial strategy improvement, depth of our experience*
Target markets: *Automobile dealerships, body shops*

Timing: *12 months*
Anticipated sales: ($ or unit; by quarter) *$5,000/year minimum fee*
Anticipated costs:
1. Development *$5,000 to $8,000*
2. Advertising *Direct mail, Telemarketing $2,000 to $3,000*
3. Impact on other products/services *Will augment client base*
4. Other (specify) _____
Comments: _____

Action taken: _____

By: _____　Date: _____

Don't hurry with any product change. Let the idea stew for a while. Discuss it. Play the devil's advocate. New products have hidden costs that are difficult to foresee, and seldom pay off as well or as fast as you hope.

Summary for Chapter Two
1. You looked at your products and services and noted the benefits they offer and the target markets who seek those benefits. Keep a copy of Figure 2.4 for reference. Update it as needed.
2. You compared your products and services to those offered by your leading competitors to determine differences and gain preliminary ideas on how to differentiate your business from theirs. Figure 2.2 will help you determine the unique selling proposition of each product or service, which will be used in setting advertising directions.
3. You looked at each major product and service to find new applications (and new target markets). Figure 2.3 is a piece of the competitive analysis puzzle, as well as a source of new product line or product mix ideas.
4. Risk analysis entered the picture in Figures 2.6 and 2.7.
5. You found competitive strengths and weaknesses in what you market. You will use this in Chapter Six to help define your competitive position.
6. You outlined new product and service objectives in Figure 2.8. You may have to work these into your sales and profit goals. New products cast long shadows.

Figure 2.9
A Summary of Your Product/Service Goals

Sales Goals (for each quarter of next year, in dollars or in units)

Product/Service:	I	II	III	IV	TOTAL
1. Business Consulting	10,000	10,000	10,000	10,000	40,000
2. Monthly accounting	10,000	10,000	10,000	10,000	40,000
3. Audits	7,500	7,500	7,500	7,500	30,000
4. Tax return prep.	20,000	2,500	5,000	2,500	30,000
5. Tax consultation & representation	7,500	7,500	7,500	7,500	30,000
6. Special Projects	7,500	7,500	7,500	7,500	30,000
7. Other accounting services	6,250	6,250	6,250	6,250	25,000

Chapter Three:
Customers and Prospects

Who wants your goods and services?

You can't know too much about your customers and prospects. This calls for marketing research. Facts and figures elevate your marketing plans from wishful thinking to purposeful action. There is no substitute for hard information.

Your hunches, based on experience and observation, are important. They simplify market research by defining limits and setting directions for further investigation.

But they have to be substantiated. Hunches have an irksome way of being half-truths, and half-truths can be disastrous. "I feel that there's a big market for this..." and "I have a hunch that we can double sales by..." are two of the most common pitfalls for small business owners. Put another way, small businesses aren't destroyed from outside by competitors or fate. Often, they self-destruct.

Your hunches have to be substantiated.

Figure 3.1
Marketing Research Samples

Marketing research provides answers to questions like:
1. Who are your best customers and prospects?
2. How does the 80/20 rule (that 80% of your profits come from 20% of your customers) affect you?
3. How do your customers perceive your products/services?
4. What do they want from a business like yours?
5. How can you profitably satisfy their needs and wants?
6. What's the potential of this market?
7. Should you market goods, services, or both?
8. What do your customers read, watch, listen to?

You have to know how your target markets perceive the value of your products/services to make good marketing decisions. If you don't know how your company and its products/services are perceived, you will waste time and aim the wrong products at the wrong markets at the wrong time.

Professional marketing consultants can get this information faster and more cheaply than you can. If your budget is tight, check with local business schools. Marketing professors sometimes do consulting work. Since most basic market research questions are the same, this saves you from reinventing the wheel. It should cost you no more than other out of pocket expenses. Marketing consultants know the questions to ask and how to get the answers. They will put this information to work, ferreting out better opportunities for you to pursue. This is an added bonus for your marketing-research investment.

Your aim is to categorize your current customers as prime, good, and others.

Figure 3.2
Basic Marketing Research Questions

These are a few questions that basic market research will help you answer.

Information about the buyer:
  Age?
  Annual income?
  Gender?
  Ethnic group?
  Profession or occupation?
  Owner of a home?
  Media preferred?

Information about the competition:
  Market share?
  Advertising plan?
  Price strategies?
  Distribution?
  Length of time in business?

Information about the product:
  Benefits?
  Price?
  Service?
  Design specifics?
  Where sold?
  Packaging?
  How will it be used?
  How many bought in a year?
  What to improve?

Question 10: Who are your current customers?
You can't specify target markets, segment the markets, or otherwise improve your marketing abilities without detailed knowledge about your current customers.

Suppose your market is limited to punk rock fans. What will you do when the next fad hits? Grow up with your market and change with them? Or cater to the tastes of adolescents forever?

If you sell to industrial companies, who are they? What are their sales levels and geographical distribution? Who makes the buying decision? What market segment buys which products—and what information can these people give you?

If you sell to individual consumers, what are they like? What are the demographics of the market? What are the people's age, gender, income, stage in the life cycle, education level?

Market segmentation is a method of organizing and categorizing those persons or organizations which you think will buy your products. Look at your customers and note their salient characteristics, then look to wider markets for more groups of people with the same (or similar) characteristics. The usual route is to begin with a fuzzy concept, seek out more detailed information to help define some rough market segments, then refine these into better defined target markets. This can be entertaining as well as highly rewarding.

The ingenuity of market research professionals is noteworthy. As an example, a research technique called VALS (for Value and Life-Style Study) was developed by the Stanford Research Institute and helped Manufacturers Hanover Trust Company in New York identify six psychographic groups within one demographic segment—the "baby boomers." (Psychographics, a valuable market analysis tool, examines the life-styles and values of various market segments to determine how consumers think and what motivates them.) The upshot was a successful marketing campaign that used only one slogan, "We realize your potential," to appeal to the six different mindsets. You might be able to benefit from describing your customers and hot prospects using the segmentation criteria in Figure 3.3 on the next page.

Put these to work for you. Figure 3.4: Market Segmentation Worksheet may be helpful. You will probably find that you sell most profitably to certain segments and very poorly to others, which should influence your planning. Think of the old 80/20 rule: 80% of your profits come from 20% of your customers. If you can get a good handle on who that profitable 20% is and who the unprofitable 80% is, you will prosper.

Figure 3.3
Some Market Segmentation Criteria

Use these categories as criteria to describe your customer base. Look for clusters of people described by these criteria to help direct further marketing efforts.

Demographic:
    Age
    Gender
    Income level
    Occupation
    Religion
    Race/ethnic group
    Education
    Social class

Geographic:
    Country
    Region
    State
    County
    City/town
    Size of population
    Climate
    Population density

Psychographic:
    Leader or follower
    Extrovert or introvert
    Achievement-oriented or content with the status quo
    Independent or dependent
    Conservative or liberal
    Traditional or experimental
    Societally-conscious or self-centered

Consumer/Behavioral:
    Rate of usage
    Benefits sought
    Method of usage
    Frequency of usage
    Frequency of purchase

Business Markets:
    Type of business (manufacturer, retail, wholesale, service)
    Standard Industrial Classification (SIC) Code
    Size of business
    Financial strength
    Number of employees
    Location
    Structure
    Sales level
    Special requirements
    Distribution patterns

Figure 3.4
Market Segmentation Worksheet

Fill out one of these forms for each of your products/services.

By: *GL* Date: *2/10/87*

Product/service: *All accounting services we offer*

Describe your "ideal customers" according to the criteria listed in Figures 3.2 and 3.3. *Entrepreneurs in their late 30s to early 50s; owners of retail, service or manufacturing firms with sales of $100,000 to $5,000,000.*

Describe their purchasing patterns. *When they are aware of their need. They want aggressive and innovative solutions to their problems — they don't have time to research solutions themselves. Often, they need special work performed.*

What makes them "ideal customers" for this product/service?

They have good ideas and want them implemented. Also, they can pay our $5,000 annual fee.

Question 11: What are their buying habits?
Who buys what, when, where, and why are key pieces of marketing information. If you determine nothing more than the answers to these questions, you will be miles ahead of most of your competitors.

Gather the following basic information on each product, product line, or service you offer:
- Who makes the buying decision?
- What's the size of the sale in dollars?
- How many units are sold?
- What is your cost per sale?
- What do your customers buy?
- When do they buy it?
- Is their purchase seasonal?
- Why do they buy it?
- Where do they make the buying decision?
- How do they finance their purchase?

How do your customers view your products and services? This is a research and development question. If you can define your products from your customers' point of view, you can discover new ways to market your products/services, new target markets, new profitability. For instance, if a customer asks for a refinement of a standard product in your line, can you redesign and repackage that product for other people?

> Who buys what, when, where, and why are key pieces of marketing information.

The key marketing point: People buy solutions to problems.

Reworking your basic products and services to fit customer demands can be a powerful marketing tool. Here are some examples:
1. Blister packaging of foods and medicines after the first Tylenol scare.
2. The ongoing simplification of microcomputers. The current generation of "user-friendly" computers is geared to people unfamiliar with computers.
3. Overnight package delivery. Federal Express spotted a market for overnight small package and letter delivery. It was always there; they just were the first to spot it. Their competitors are still playing catch-up.
4. Cash management accounts. They opened huge markets for Merrill Lynch and should have been developed by the banking industry. However, the bankers just didn't notice that their customers' problems juggling various banking and brokerage accounts had created a mammoth opportunity.

The key marketing point: People buy solutions to problems. They buy satisfaction of their wants and needs. They don't buy products and services. If your customers have complaints, find out why. What's their problem? How can your company help them solve that problem?

Question 12: Why do your customers buy your goods/services?
Answer this one correctly and become rich and famous.

How can you find out why people buy from you? Ask them. (Figure 3.5 on the next page is a survey R.C. Montville and Company, CPAs, used for their clients. A generic version of Figure 3.5 appears in *The Market Planning Guide Workbook*.) It helps if you give your customers a structure. This is an area where a professionally developed survey pays off. Call your local SBA office and ask for the nearest Small Business Institute program. Check with local colleges—a customer survey is one of those projects that costs you little and gains you a lot.

When you do a survey make sure to get answers to these three basic questions:
1. Where did you hear of our store/product/service?
2. What would you like us to offer?
3. How can we better serve you?

In Figure 2.4, you matched products with the needs and wants they fulfill. Now put those insights to work. Who has these needs and wants? Which of your target markets can you satisfy profitably? Maybe you can reposition some of your products to appeal to these markets. Maybe you will have to change the product/service mix.

The important thing to keep in mind is that people won't buy goods and services they don't want, no matter how good the advertising and positioning. You can only sell them what they want to buy. Sometimes that will be what they need. But it will very seldom be what you think you are selling.

Some examples: You think you sell a medical service. Your customers think they are buying a solution to a problem, a friendly ear, an antidote to fear. Helena Rubenstein was widely quoted as saying she didn't sell perfume, she sold hope. Detroit sells transportation, not cars. Hollywood sells entertainment, not movies.

More examples: If you sell to bureaucrats, remember that their number one concern is to be safe. If you sell to teenagers, remember they need to be in step with their peers. If you sell to a local retail customer base, remember that they buy convenience, safety, cleanliness, and courtesy along with your groceries or dry goods.

Apply this way of thinking to your business. What emotional needs or wants do your products satisfy? What other benefits do they provide? Then match those benefits to your target markets.

How can you determine your market's needs and wants? Ask them. Observe them. Read—trade magazines are full of articles about why people buy, and what triggers their purchasing decisions. Attend trade seminars. Talk with other business owners and managers. Above all, ask your customers.

Figure 3.5
R.C. Montville and Company's Client Survey

To our valued clients:

Please take a few minutes to complete this short questionnaire. Our aim is to give you the service you need, want and deserve. Your honest answers to these questions can help us serve you better.

1. How would you rate the quality of work we have performed for you in the past?

    Excellent _____   Good _____   Fair _____   Poor _____

    1A. If not excellent, please explain.
    _____
    _____

2. How would you rate the timeliness of the work we perform for you?

    Excellent _____   Good _____   Fair _____   Poor _____

    2A. If not excellent, please explain.
    _____
    _____

3. What service would you like us to perform for you that we do not offer?
    _____
    _____

4. Please feel free to give us any constructive criticism you feel we could use.
    _____
    _____

5. We plan to begin a seminar series in the not too distant future. What areas would you like to see covered in these seminars?
    _____
    _____

    5A. How interested would you be in attending our seminars?

    Very _____   Somewhat _____   Little _____   Not at all _____

Remember why you're in business: to create customers and satisfy them, at an acceptable profit.

Question 13: Who are your best customers and prospects?
Use a straightforward approach: Match the information about the most profitable products with the market segments that purchase those products. If you can figure out why they made these purchases and can find other groups in sufficient numbers with similar characteristics, then these new groups become your best prospects. With luck, they will turn into your best customers.

This is an endless process. Your target markets change over time; your product lines and mix change; your business changes.

But the basic process remains constant:
1. Identify your profitable products/services, including the "rising stars."
2. Find out as much as you can about the people who buy those products/services. Who are they? What are their buying patterns? How often do they buy? How much do they spend? What offers do they respond to?
3. Find other people like them. These are your hot prospects.
4. Identify unprofitable products/services, including the "dogs" and "owner's ego."
5. Find out who buys these products/services—and stop marketing to them, or switch them to more profitable products. This may mean leaving a comfortable market for a profitable one. Remember why you're in business: to create customers and satisfy them, at an acceptable profit.

Question 14: What is your market share?
Market share is the percentage share of total sales to a given market. For example, if you sell $225,000 worth of medical services annually to a market which buys $1,000,000 worth of that particular service a year, you'd have a 22.5% market share. Market share can be measured in unit sales: 225,000 units out of a total market of 1,000,000 units. Or in purchasing units: 225,000 people out of the total market of 1,000,000 buy your product.

Note that market share presupposes knowledge of the total size of the market, which depends in turn on how you define your target market.

Market share information helps you decide whether to enter, abandon, invade, or protect a market niche. As a rule of thumb, a 25% market share is dominant and makes you a major player in that market. If you can identify a market niche large enough for profitability, yet small enough to be unattractive to big businesses, and grab 25% of that market, you have a winner. On the other hand, if your archrival has 50% of that market, there might not be room for both of you.

Question 14A: Is your market share growing, shrinking, or stable?
Question 14B: Is the market growing, shrinking, or stable? Is it changing in other ways?
A declining market may be a good one to bail out of, or may present a terrific niche possibility. A growing market may be an opportunity for you to develop a growing niche. It could also present an enticing market to a large company which could swamp the market.

Market-share information is one of many factors involved in these kinds of strategic choices. You have to use your judgment. And remember that judgment based on facts beats guesswork.

Judgment based on facts beats guesswork.

Summary for Chapter Three
1. You have segmented your customer base (Figure 3.4).
2. You know (based on your research) why these people buy your products/services, and what needs or wants they satisfy.
3. This helps you form a clear, easily communicated description of the target markets to which you can market effectively.
4. You can now set realistic target market objectives to include in your marketing plan, including the size of your markets, your market share goals, and other precise measures of performance. Fill out Figure 3.6 in your *Market Planning Guide Workbook*.

Sample objectives might be to enter some niches, to try to attract certain market segments while dropping efforts to attract others, or to work on certain product lines that sell to current customers. You have to remember your own business situation and that these objectives are based on facts and analysis, not wishful thinking.

Figure 3.6
Customer/Prospect Summary Form

By: _OL_   Date: _2/10/87_

Reviewed by: _____   Date: _____

These are our most valuable customers and prospects, ranked from the top:
(Make sure you list the market segments and their criteria.)

   Name of Customer   Market Segment   Criteria (See Figure 3.3)
1. _ABC Co._ — _40s, affluent, manufacturers, aggressive_
2. _DEF Co._ — _40s, wealthy, service, aggressive_
3. _GHI Co._ — _40s, wealthy, manufacturers, aggressive_
4. _____
5. _____

We should target these prospects:

   Name of Prospect   Market Segment   Criteria (See Figure 3.3)
1. _XYZ Body Shop_ — _auto_ ⎫ _Sales of $700,000+/year;_
2. _JML's Tires_ — _auto_ ⎬ _in business for at_
3. _Granite State Dodge_ — _auto_ ⎭ _least 5 years_
4. _____
5. _____

We should consider these market niches:

1. _Manufacturers of microwave components_
2. _Sporting goods retailers_
3. _Consultants and consulting companies_
4. _____
5. _____

Our customer/prospect objectives for the next year are:

1. _Penetrate auto-related markets_
2. _Upgrade prospects/customers to $1,000,000 sales_
3. _Focus! Focus! Focus!!_

Chapter Four:
Competitive Analysis

In Chapter One, Question 5, you made a list of obstacles which might impede achieving your goals. One of the biggest impediments is the competition. No business operates in a competitive vacuum, and there are plenty of other smart business owners looking to your target markets for their next sale.

Business is competitive. Customers' needs and expectations shift. New products and different services fight for consumers' dollars. New players enter the market while others leave it.

What can you do about the competition? Plenty. Think of the comprehensive scouting reports that major league managers rely on. They carefully observe their competitors. They study everything about them that could possibly affect the outcome of a game. They know who the players are, what their strong and weak points might be, what strategies they use, what they tend to do in a pinch, what resources they can call on, and other information. You need at least as much information about your competitors.

Competitive analysis is an important part of your marketing plan. You can learn from your competitors and strengthen your business. You can predict their plans if you observe them closely. This takes work and close attention to detail. Most small business owners approach competitive analysis haphazardly. Set up a structured approach (think of major league baseball again) and seize a whopping competitive advantage.

Question 15: Who are your competitors?
Anyone who sells similar products/services in your marketplace, or similar products/services in other marketplaces, or who could sell similar products/services is a competitor. You compete for your target market's time and money. In the advertising cliché, you want to gain their Attention, Interest, Desire, and Action (the mnemonic is AIDA)—but so do a lot of competing businesses.

Competitive analysis begins with identifying your immediate competition: Who are your five leading competitors?

As you fine-tune your analysis of the competition, you will want to add the less direct competition.

Future competitors may be the most threatening if you are in a highly desirable, rapidly growing market. But for most small business owners, just staying on top of the current market will be enough.

Remember: You aren't the only smart business owner out there. If you learn from your competitors, they can learn from you.

> **No business operates in a competitive vacuum, and there are plenty of other smart business owners looking to your target markets for their next sale.**

Business is competitive, and you have to scout out the competition.

Figure 4.1
Our Competitors

By: _GL_ Date: _2/11/87_

My closest competitors are:

1. _Bridge & Silverman_
2. _S, B & R_
3. _Purdy, Borenstein_
4. _____
5. _____

Other competitors (include potential as well as actual) are:

1. _Bigelow & Company_
2. _"Big Eight" Accounting Firms_
3. _____

You have to learn a lot about your competition before you can make useful comparisons. Remember the major league scouting reports. A scout will follow a team for weeks, making copious observations on each player. Can he hit a curve? How about the shortstop's ability to go to his right? Do they use the hit-and-run, or prefer sacrifice bunts in the late innings? The scouting is organized, thorough, and professionally executed. Otherwise it's not sufficiently informative.

Business is competitive, and you have to scout out the competition. This may seem like spying. It is. A spy has to have some idea of his or her objectives. So do you. The information you gather should have a purpose and a structure that is updated periodically. This information sets your marketing strategies.

Use Figure 4.2: Competitor Information to organize your scouting reports. Much of the information is readily available from Dun & Bradstreet and other publicly available reports. Your banker can get this information for you, or you can piece it together yourself. Fill in these forms for each serious competitor, and keep the forms on file. Over a year or so you will develop a most informative dossier on your competition.

This is an area where knowledge is power. For many of us, the problem is gaining that knowledge. There are few shortcuts—but the process is simple enough. You build the dossier piece by piece, over time, using the competition's advertising, press releases, promotional materials of all kinds, your own observations, and comments from vendors, customers, employees, friends, and your business advisors. As the file grows, you will know enough about your competitors to anticipate their moves, learn from their strengths and weaknesses, and increase your competitive advantage.

Don't feel badly about doing this. Your stronger competitors are doing this with you already.

Figure 4.2
Competitor Information

Prepared by: _OL_ Date: _2/11/87_

Competitor: _S, B & R_

Product/service: _Tax preparation and accounting services_

Location(s): _Portsmouth_

Specific information:

    Years in business: _24_

    Number of employees: _20_

    Dollar sales: _$3,000,000_

    Unit sales: _____

    Market share: _Approximately 20%_

    Financial strength: _Excellent_

    Profitability: _?_

Players (include their ages, experience in this business, training or education, strengths and weaknesses, and other pertinent information):

    President/owner: _____

    Outside advisors: _____

    Key employees: _____

The competition's marketing strategy:

    Pricing: _Accounting services: low   Taxes: high_

    Advertising themes: _none_

    Promotion/public relations efforts: _____

Significant changes (new people, products, etc.): _____

How this competitor competes with you: _More conservative_

Comments: _I need to do more research to finish this!_

Your top competitors look at your business for ideas. Do the same to theirs.

Do your competitors see a weakness in your business or a market potential you missed? Your top competitors look at your business for ideas. Do the same to theirs. Your aim is to find out how you stack up against your competition. What are their strengths relative to yours? Where do you differ?

Many businesses go beyond scouting the competition. They have themselves scouted ("shopped") in order to have an unbiased appraisal of how they measure up against the competition.

Some questions you might want to raise are:
1. How are your competitors financed?
2. Can they raise more money? A division of a larger company, for example, has a potential advantage over a small business in this area.
3. Are they heavily in debt? This would make price competition dangerous to them.
4. Are they investing in new products or services? Why?
5. What training do they give their personnel? Small business owners are notoriously unwilling to provide adequate training. This can be exploited.
6. What image (if any) are they trying to develop?
7. What are their target markets?
8. Do they compete on price, quality, service, or convenience?

Question 16: What do your competitors do better than you?
Question 17: What do you do better than your competitors?
One application of Figure 4.2 is to alert you to your competitors' strengths and weaknesses relative to your business.

Maybe they have a better product, a more motivated sales force, or better cost and quality controls which result in a price advantage. Maybe they have a superior location or a better distribution system. Or perhaps they are instituting a strong sales training program.

Once you know what their strengths are, learn from them. Avoid their weaknesses in your own business, but be ready to attack them with your marketing strategies. There usually is little difference between one small business and another. Those little differences, though, are what separate a profitable, enjoyable business from struggling businesses.

Use Figures 4.3 and 4.4 as guidelines.

In Figure 4.3: Comparing Yourself to Competitors, write down what your competition is doing in the five principal comparison areas. Then, in the last column, jot down how you stack up in these areas.

Figure 4.3
Comparing Yourself to Your Competitors

Prepared by: _QL_   Date: _2/11/87_

Competitor: _S, B & R_

	Describe your competitor's:	How do you stack up?
Price	High	Lower, but headed up
Quality	OK	Even better
Service	OK	Even better
Location	Good	Poor—we are changing to a better one
Advertising	None	Aggressive
Other yardsticks	Been around a long time	Relatively new

The other yardsticks might be product lines, staffing, sales practices, or whatever you find to be important competitive information for your business. But you have to know how you compare on the other listed items to differentiate your company from the competition.

All five major yardsticks are far more detailed than you may at first think. For example, consider advertising.

Look carefully at all of the competitor's advertising. What are they trying to say? Do they feature price, delivery, or reliability? Do they focus on one strength—for example, technical skill or convenience? How important do you think their advertised benefits are to the targeted market? Where do they advertise—trade journals? Radio or newspaper? Billboards? Is their advertising more effective than yours? Should you review your advertising?

Figure 4.4: Quick Comparison provides a list of comparisons based on what your customers are looking for. If you have been listening to your market, this form can provide valuable insights for your marketing strategies—and provide more ways to differentiate your business from the others.

Your marketing strategy should be based on your strengths, the competition's weaknesses, and the market's desires.

Figure 4.4

Quick Comparison—Benefits Offered to Our Customers

Customer seeks:	Competitor offers	We offer
Quality		
Exclusivity		
✓ Lower prices		Ours lower than competition
Product line		
✓ Product service	Depends on size of account	More handholding
Reliability		
✓ Delivery		Always meet deadlines
✓ Location	Downtown	Easy access; will visit clients
✓ Information	Newsletter	News releases & seminars
✓ Availability		Always when needed, including evenings and weekends
Credit cards		
Credit line		
✓ Warranty		If not satisfied, client pays no fee
✓ Customer advice		Always provided
Accessories		
✓ Knowledgeability		Take courses every year
Polite help		

Your marketing strategy should be based on your strengths, the competition's weaknesses, and the market's desires.

Shore up weak areas in your business to become more competitive. This can pay off fast. For example, if analysis shows that you have surly clerks and a dingy store while the competitors have trained their clerks to be polite and provide a clean, well-lighted, spacious store, your first move would be to clean house. The next step would be to advertise the change widely and build on whatever strengths you originally had. Think of how the auto parts industry changed in response to competitive pressures from large stores such as Sears and K-Mart. The mechanics' macho havens are on the way out, and newer stores (ADAP for one) have carved out a highly profitable niche by changing the image of auto parts stores.

Question 18: What is your competitive position?
Locate yourself on the competitive continuum in Figure 4.5. A visual reminder of where you are helps stimulate and motivate your employees in the same way that knowing your position in a league helps you knuckle down to improve your own skills.

Figure 4.5
Competitive Continuum

Strong ____+____|____-____Weak

Where are you located on this continuum? What are you going to do about it?

How do you rank relative to the competition in these areas? A '+' means you are stronger than the competition, a '-' means you are weaker.

	Strong ____+____|____-____Weak
Finances	— (weak)
Marketing	— (weak)
Pricing	+
Selling	+
Production	+
Distribution	
Training	—
Personnel	— (weak)

Summary for Chapter Four
1. You have identified your competition and have begun to collect detailed information on them (Figures 4.1 and 4.2).
2. You know your relative competitive position, based on a careful assessment of your leading competitors (Figure 4.5).
3. You know how you stack up against the competition on some specific points, which helps establish strategic directions on the "build on your strengths and attack their weaknesses" principle (Figures 4.3 and 4.4).
4. This gives you the information to set realistic and attainable competitive objectives for the next year. Figure 4.6: Competitive Objectives summarizes these goals. You will be referring back to Figure 4.6 in your marketing plan.

These objectives don't need to be detailed here. You will consider other aspects of your competitive position before writing your final marketing plan. While these preliminary objectives are very important as indicators for your planning, they will most likely be substantially modified by the time you flesh them out.

Figure 4.6
Competitive Objectives

Prepared by: _GL_ Date: _2/11/87_

Reviewed by: _____ Date: _____

We need to improve our competitive position in these areas:
1. _Finances_
2. _Marketing_
3. _Training our personnel_

We can build on our competitive strengths in these areas:
1. _Selling_
2. _Production_
3. _Personnel_

We can attack our competition in their weak areas:
1. _Service_
2. _Offer business consulting in addition to accounting services_
3. _____

Chapter Five:
Price, Location, and Sales Practices

Three of the most important (and difficult to establish) pieces of your marketing plan are price (how to set prices to maximize profits and achieve other goals), location (where you do business, including distribution patterns), and sales practices (how you sell your products).

Within limits, these are fixed. Prices are somewhat determined by market conditions and competition. Where you open shop may already be established, but can be changed. Distribution patterns and delivery routes depend on sales patterns and customer demand. Sales practices are perhaps the hardest patterns to change, and cause the most problems.

However, you do have some latitude in each of these areas. You don't have to play follow-the-leader, or put up with an inadequate location or inept sales practices. You can change them to your benefit and competitive advantage.

Question 19: How do you establish prices?
The dilemma is whether to aim for high volume/low prices (the Woolworth five-and-ten route) or low volume/high prices (à la Tiffany's).

This is complicated by the way your markets react to price changes. Does a small price rise lead to a large drop in unit sales, or does a big price rise lead to a negligible drop in unit sales? This sensitivity to price changes is called "price elasticity" and studies are often available through industry or trade associations. If your trade association doesn't have such studies, try sampling small segments of your markets. Your local college may be able to conduct an elasticity study for you, which has the additional benefit of shielding you from customers who may be highly price sensitive. Students conducting surveys can get away with more than you can in this delicate area.

Keep in mind that all pricing policies are competitive. Knowing how sensitive your target markets are to price change puts you at an advantage over firms which follow a reactive pricing policy, but there are many other factors to keep in mind.

To set your pricing policy, follow these five steps:
1. *Define your pricing objectives.* Tie these to your overall marketing and business goals (see Figures 1.3 and 1.5).

Some common pricing objectives include maintaining or building market share, maximizing profits or return on investment, meeting competition, introducing new products, increasing sales, or all of these.

All pricing policies are competitive.

Knowledge beats guesswork every time.

Figure 5.1
Pricing Factors

PRICE = Image + Service + Product + Overhead + Profit
These influence pricing policies:
1. *Price sensitivity* (elasticity).
2. *Quality.* High quality and high prices often go together.
3. *Product differentiation.* High differentiation and high prices, and low differentiation (commodity products) and low prices, often go together.
4. *Competition.* Competitive markets and price chopping as a market share strategy go together.
5. *Service.* The more service you provide, the higher the price. A fully assembled, carefully chosen bicycle from a cycle shop costs more than the same bike bought disassembled from an outlet store.
6. *Location.* Stores on Rodeo Drive command higher prices than those located in local shopping malls.
7. *Target markets.* Some markets buy on price. A low price can scare people off ("The price is so low—what's wrong with this?") or be an excellent marketing tool. Know your markets.
8. *Marketing objectives.* Are you looking for market share? Profits? New markets? Your objectives must be reflected in your price strategies.
9. *Your business costs.* Your pricing has to reflect your business, not someone else's.

Perceived value to customers = Product + Intangibles (service, quality are examples) + Specialized expertise

---

2. Establish price ranges. This is complicated, so call in your accountant or financial advisors. Three questions to raise when setting price ranges are:

A. *What is your break-even point?* (See Figure 5.2.) This establishes the low end of the acceptable range. You must at least meet your expenses (break even) before you can make a profit. Can you reach your breakeven point given sales forecasts and current prices? How far can you exceed it?

B. *What are your profit goals?* If you can't reach the profit goals given unit sales forecasts and acceptable prices, you might want to rethink your strategies, or market more aggressively. (See Figures 1.5 and 2.9.)

C. *How do your target markets perceive your products/services?* This includes questions of price sensitivity as well as product differentiation. Oddly enough, the small business scourge "lack of courage in pricing" often stems from not knowing how the market perceives the value of products and services. Don't guess here. Use surveys, questionnaires, market research, and trade studies. Knowledge beats guesswork every time. This piece of knowledge helps you establish the upper limit of your price range. Sometimes this is called "what the market will bear."

Fill out Figure 5.3 in your *Market Planning Workbook* for each product/service or each product/service line. Save these forms for future review.

Figure 5.2
Break-Even Analysis

Break-even analysis pinpoints where revenue equals total costs. To calculate your break-even point, take your most current income statement and identify each cost as either fixed or variable. Fixed costs are independent of sales level, while variable costs rise and fall with sales. Mixed costs involve elements of both. Most costs will fall readily into fixed or variable. For those that don't, allocate 50% to fixed costs, and 50% to variable.

Fixed Expenses:	Variable Expenses:
Salaries	Sales commissions
Payroll tax	Sales tax
Benefits	Boxes, paper, etc.
Utilities	Travel
Licenses and fees	Freight
Insurance	Overtime
Advertising	Bad debts
Legal and accounting	
Depreciation	Mixed:
Interest	Telephone
Maintenance and cleaning	Postage

The break-even formula is:

$$BE = F/(S-V)$$

where BE = break-even sales in dollars
F = fixed costs in dollars
S = sales expressed as 100%
V = variable costs as a percentage of sales

If F = $10,000, S = 100%, and V = 50%, then BE = ($10,000/50%) = $20,000.

In other words, costs will exceed revenue until you have sold $20,000 worth of goods.

Figure 5.3
Price Range Guidelines

By: _GL_ Date: _2/12/87_

Product/Service: _All accounting services_

Price range: $ _40/hr_ to $ _75/hr_

1. Price floor:

    (a) Markon (gross margin) is _____ % of retail price.
    (b) Manufacturer's suggested price is $ _____.
    (c) Fixed costs are $ _____. Variable costs are $ _____ or _____ % of sales.
    (d) Breakeven is $ _____.

2. Special considerations for this product's price are:

    ☑ Service
    ☐ Status
    ☑ Quality
    ☐ Loss leader
    ☐ Demand
    ☐ Product life
    ☐ Overhead
    ☐ Downtime
    ☐ Competition
    ☐ Market penetration costs
    ☐ Other (specify):

    Something to think about: Our fees can be higher if the client's perception of value is raised!

3. Turnover rate is _____ times per year. _Not applicable_

4. Industry turn average is _____ times per year. "

5. Going rate is _$50 to $100/hr_

6. I estimate _____ units will be sold. _Not applicable_

7. _31_ _hours/week_ (number of units) at $ _75/hr._ will cover my fixed costs.

8. Top price possible is $ _____. (This estimate is based on the customer's perception of value.)

Comments:

3. *Define competitive pricing strategy.* See Figure 5.4 for some ideas. Since all pricing strategies are competitive, a major factor in your choice will be what the other guys are doing. This doesn't mean that you want to follow them. It does mean that you want to know what they are doing so you can defeat them in the marketplace.

> **Your price strategies have to reflect your business's cost structures and profit goals, not someone else's.**

Figure 5.4
Price Setting Thoughts

Consider setting prices above your competitor's prices if:
- ☐ Your market is not sensitive to price changes.
- ☐ Your market consists mainly of growing businesses.
- ☐ Your product is an integral part of an established system.
- ☐ Your reputation for status, service, and other positive perceptions in the market increases your products' perceived value.
- ☐ Your customers can easily build your price into their selling price.
- ☐ Your product is only a tiny percentage of your customers' total costs.

Consider setting your prices just below your competition if:
- ☐ Your market is sensitive to price changes.
- ☐ You're attempting to enter a new market.
- ☐ Your customers need to reorder parts or supplies.
- ☐ Your business is small enough that a lower price won't cause your larger competitors to start a price war.
- ☐ You have the option of economical production or purchasing which decreases your unit cost.
- ☐ You have not reached full production capacity.

---

4. *Consider the impact of product lines, inventory costs, and selling costs.* Sometimes you have to flesh out a product line to meet other competitive pressures and rather than carry the product forever, you decide to turn it over even at a loss. Inventory costs are a hidden burden on many retail businesses (ask your accountant) and can drive up your short-term borrowing needs.

Some businesses find that sales costs are the dominant pricing factor. Think of encyclopedia sales, where everyone from the door-to-door salesperson on up gets a commission. The $600 price is based on a minimal product cost, plus a substantial research and development cost, plus a staggering sales cost.

Keep your costs in mind when setting prices. Your price strategies have to reflect your business's cost structures and profit goals, not someone else's.

5. *Choose a flexible pricing strategy.* Every industry has its own favorite pricing strategy, and you should use your industry pattern as a guide.

> **Set firm price ranges for each product/service or product/service line, keep an eye open for competitive moves, and check constantly to ensure that your prices serve your profit and other marketing objectives.**

The four main methods of determining price are:

A. *Suggested or going rate.* This is the least defensible method, since it removes your business from the pricing decision. This is far and away the most common method: It is simple. It takes no work. It also is almost totally ineffective.

B. *Full-cost pricing.* Full-costing may be appropriate if you can identify all your operating costs, then distribute them over merchandise costs, add a preset profit, and crank out the prices. One weakness of this method is that the merchandise has to be sold, and in sufficient quantities to push you past the break-even point. Another more glaring weakness is that full-cost pricing presupposes that your accounting system is able to capture all the costs and make accurate forecasts.

The advantage is that full-cost pricing makes pricing simple. It is most helpful as a guideline, and can help narrow the price ranges set earlier.

C. *Gross margin.* This can be figured either as a markup (adding a percentage of wholesale cost to your base cost) or as a markon (percent of the retail price represented by the gross margin).

This method takes operating costs and market factors into account, but is only as good as your ability to meet projected sales levels. The big advantage is that gross-margin pricing helps set uniform price floors. You can then change prices to reflect market conditions, the market's sensitivity to price change, competition, and so on.

D. *Flexible markups.* This is less rigid than full-costing, and is particularly helpful during periods of fluctuating prices. It demands that you have information about your market's sensitivity to price changes.

The main weakness of this approach is that it is all too easy to pursue sales at the expense of profit. While you don't want to hold on to inventory too long, you don't want to give it away either. This is a problem most merchants have to grapple with.

The best method of all is to combine the strengths of these four methods. Set firm price ranges for each product/service or product/service line, keep an eye open for competitive moves, and check constantly to ensure that your prices serve your profit and other marketing objectives. Whatever you do, don't slap a price on your products and refuse to change it when conditions change. Rigidity is as great a danger as being totally reactive to every market whim.

Try to ascertain factual answers to the questions in Figure 5.5 when you set pricing policies.

Figure 5.5
Pricing Checklist

Estimating demand:
1. Which products/services do customers shop around for?
2. Which products/services are in greater demand even at higher prices?
3. Are certain products/services in greater demand at one time of the year than another? If so, which? And what is the duration of that demand?
4. Do your customers expect a certain price range?
5. What is the balance between price and quality in your market?

The competition:
1. What are your competitors' pricing strategies?
2. Are your prices based on an average gross margin consistent with your competitors'?
3. Is your policy to sell consistently at a higher price, lower price, or at the same price as your competitors? Why?
4. How do your competitors respond to your prices?

Pricing and market share:
1. What is your present market share?
2. What are your market share goals? To increase share? Maintain share?
3. What effect will price changes have on your market share?
4. Is your production capacity consistent with your market share goals?

Strategy:
1. Have you determined how pricing affects your sales/volume goals?
2. How can pricing help you gain new business?
3. Have you tested the impact of price strategies on your markets?
4. Are your strategies in line with broader economic trends?

Policies:
1. How does the nature of your products affect their price?
2. How does your method of distribution affect price?
3. Do your promotional policies affect prices?

> The three most important factors in retail business are location, location, and location.

Question 20: How does your location affect you?
According to Small Business Administration studies, the most common reason to pick a new business site is "noticed vacancy." Since the three most important factors in retail business are location, location, and location, it is no surprise that many small businesses never reach their potential.

If you are already in business, you still have to keep track of your trading area. Maybe you're considering a move to a new location, or building a branch office. New roads are constructed. Populations shift, zoning ordinances are altered, competitors come and go. If you can identify the advantages and disadvantages of your location, you can do something about them.

The marketing challenge is: How do you evaluate the strengths and weaknesses of your location (actual or proposed)? While some businesses don't have to worry much about location, most do. If location is important to you, get answers to these four questions:

1. *What is the traffic flow at the site?* Exposure to pedestrian and vehicle traffic will affect sales and advertising. See Figure 5.6 for some ideas.

Figure 5.6
Traffic Counts

You need two traffic counts, one for pedestrians and one for vehicular traffic. You should find out:
- ☐ How many people pass by during your business hours
- ☐ When they pass by
- ☐ Who these people are
- ☐ Where they are from
- ☐ What their shopping plans might be
- ☐ How many are logical prospects for your products or services
- ☐ If there are seasonal or other predictable fluctuations
- ☐ Where they currently buy your kind of products or services

These pieces of information help you to evaluate your site. Your advertising and other promotional programs need this information too.

---

2. *What are the other stores or offices in the area?* Complementary businesses help. It's no accident that there are clusters of stores in almost every city. Automobile alleys, fast food restaurants, and department stores are three such clusters. Shopping malls are ideal for some businesses; others prefer stand-alone sites. Every major hospital is surrounded by health-industry related small businesses: doctors' offices, pharmacies, nursing homes, and so forth.

Unless you have very good reasons to do otherwise, find out where businesses similar to yours tend to be located and join the trend. Trade associations, industry publications, and your own observations can help here.

Transitional areas pose a special opportunity and challenge. In many cities, for example, the downtown areas are coming back after years of blight. Ask the local realtors, your Chamber of Commerce, bankers, city officials, and regional planners what's happening. They all will have good ideas and suggestions for you to evaluate and perhaps act on.

3. *How's the parking?* Is the site easily accessible? Safe? Convenient? Unless you have a downtown location where parking is of no concern, this is a big question. It doesn't matter what the traffic count is if people can't find close, adequate, safe parking.

4. *What costs are involved?* Rent = Space Costs + Advertising. A poor location will compel you to spend more on advertising, while a great location allows you to spend less. As examples, shopping center rents are high, but the traffic flow in a good one justifies the cost. A low rent, while appealing, will be offset by increased advertising costs. The totals may be the same.

A poor location will compel you to spend more on advertising, while a great location allows you to spend less.

Figure 5.7
Site Evaluation

By: _GL_ Date: _2/15/87_

1. How *does* the site affect your business? _Not too much — our business is generated by word of mouth and ads._
2. How does the appearance of the building affect your business? _It's OK — successful and professional looking and not too plush._
3. Does the store's or office's appearance complement your business's image? _It doesn't hurt._
4. Do you (or can you) use the location to your best advantage? How? _Our office is easy to find._
5. Should you move or consider moving? Why? _Not yet._
6. Is the neighborhood changing? If so, how? How will it affect your business? _Yes — businesses and the local economy are growing._
7. Is the site high- or low-rent? _Moderate._
8. Is the rent competitive for the area? _Yes._
9. If your site is low-rent, how will you attract customers?
10. Is the location good from a competitive viewpoint? _It's ok — maybe we should think about moving downtown?_
11. Is the traffic sufficient for your sales objectives? _Not applicable._
12. Will neighboring stores help draw customers? _" "_
13. Is parking adequate? Would paying for customer parking make sense? _Yes._
14. Can you develop additional traffic? How? _Not applicable._
15. What disadvantages does the site have? How will you overcome them? _None._
16. Is this the best site available for your business? If no, why not? _It is adequate for now._

Examining and improving selling methods is part of your marketing plan.

Question 21: What are your sales practices?
Don't assume that your current method is the only way you can move product/service.

Examining and improving selling methods is part of your marketing plan.

1. *How are you currently selling your products/services?* For example, a medical service might be sold solely by referral from a local hospital or by word of mouth—or through more assertive methods. Most stores rely on location plus advertising in local media.

You might be able to add sales through direct mail, using sales representatives, or "belly-to-belly" selling. What changes might result in more sales? Are you cross-selling to your current customers or merely taking orders?

2. *What are your competitors' selling practices?* If they are adding salespeople, or changing their advertising strategies, or moving to a new location, better take note. How do they get new customers and retain old ones?

"Shop" the competition, either in person or by using a consultant who will provide a detailed analysis of their sales methods. While you're at it, have your own business "shopped." Close to 75% of lost customers complain of rude, discourteous, or poorly informed salespersons—and the irate customer complains to an average of 11 other people. That's powerful negative word-of-mouth.

3. *What follow-up do you have after the sale?* Your best prospects are your current customers. If you don't provide adequate service after the sale, that customer will end up buying from your competition.

If you never have repeat customers as part of your marketing strategy, fine. But for 99% of businesses, repeat sales are vitally important (and frequently overlooked in the scramble for new customers). Since you buy customers with your advertising and promotion efforts as well as with your products and services, it makes sense to hang on to them as long as possible.

How should you follow up? Direct mail is excellent and can be low-cost. Phone calls are good. Maintain a service desk or a call-in number. Set a strong return policy favorable to the customer.

Follow-up differentiates your business from all the others. Satisfied customers talk. So do unhappy customers. Think of the effort Sears puts into its service department. Think of how a good auto dealer provides after-sales service, or how L.L. Bean handles customer returns.

4. *What kind of sales training do you provide?* Salespeople aren't born knowing how to sell, and while you may be able to impart all the product knowledge they need, sales training is a highly specialized field.

If you don't provide sales training, why not? If it's on the grounds that sales training is an expense that you'd rather not incur, you can count on being swamped by your competitors.

Figure 5.8
"Shopping" the Competition

By: OL   Date: 2/15/87

Competitor: JB&R

Location: Portsmouth

Rate 1 (poor) to 5 (excellent)	Rating	Comments
1. Appearance and design of store	5	They've been around for a long time, and they are well-known. Also, they have a very good location.
2. Employees' characteristics:		
A. Telephone manners	4	
B. Courtesy	4	
C. Helpfulness	4	
D. Appearance	5	
E. Product knowledge	4	
F. Ability to handle complaints	3	
G. Ability to cross-sell	4	
3. Availability of products	4	
4. Convenience of location	5	
5. Added services (delivery, etc.)	4	
6. Other (specify):		

Summary for Chapter Five
1. Pricing objectives are set, and a pricing policy that serves the sales, profit, and marketing goals of your company has been considered.
2. Your location has been analyzed (Figure 5.7).
3. Sales practices—including training—have been examined, and your competitors "shopped" to ascertain their sales strengths and weaknesses (Figure 5.8).

Figure 5.9
Pricing Objectives

By: *GL*　　　　　　　　　Date: *2/15/87*

Product/Service: *Explanation of client's financial statements*

Refer to Figures 5.3, 5.4, and 5.5, and fill out one of these forms for each product/service.

My pricing objectives are	This objective will accomplish	My time frame for reaching this objective is
1. To charge an average of $200-300/month	A "door opener" for more business	Right now
2.		
3.		
4.		
5.		

Figure 5.10
Sales Practice Objectives

By: *GL*　　　　　　　　　Date: *2/15/87*

Product/Service: *All accounting services*

My sales practice objectives are	This objective will accomplish	My time frame for reaching this objective is
1. Focus on the auto industry	Make us experts for that trade; we'll get referrals, too	1 year
2. Develop local market	Save us time on the highway	Right now
3. Attend sales training program	Improve our skills	6 months
4.		

Chapter Six:
Strengths and Weaknesses

Your marketing strategy has to reflect the strengths and weaknesses of your business. This includes the competitive strengths and weaknesses noted in Chapter Four.

In a successful business, all important parts of running the business are covered adequately if not necessarily brilliantly. No major area can be left unattended. A management audit (see Figures 6.1 and 6.2) helps you gauge the quality of your management, spot areas where improvement is needed, and make sure that there are no glaring omissions to trip you up.

Your aim is to establish the right balance for your business. Your business is an assembly of systems, each of which has to work well for the whole business to be profitable. The audit helps make sure that your business has all its necessary parts, that they are all working together toward the same goals, and that the goals are suitable for the resources of your business.

Further, all parts should be the right size. A small business danger is letting one part outgrow the rest, which leads to an imbalanced allocation of resources. As you conduct your management audit, which should take only an hour or so to complete, keep balance in mind.

Any item which is checked "no" warrants your immediate attention, since it flags a weakness in your business. While a "yes" answer affirms that the area in question is at least covered, there could still be room for improvement. You may want to go over Figure 6.1 in your *Market Planning Guide Workbook* again looking for "yes" areas that you can improve on. Remember: Build on strengths, shore up weaknesses.

Your marketing strategy has to reflect the strengths and weaknesses of your business.

Figure 6.1
Management Audit

By: __OL__   Date: __2/19/87__

Based upon your analysis of the business, the operation is being run satisfactorily in the area of:

	Yes	No

I. Sales and Marketing
  A. Pricing
     Are prices in line with current industry practice? ✓
     Is your pricing policy based on your cost structure? ✓
     Have you conducted price sensitivity studies? ✓ (No)

  B. Market research
     Have you identified target markets? ✓ (some)
     Do you segment your markets? ✓ (No)
     Have you identified customer wants/needs? ✓ (No)
     Do you know how your markets perceive your products/services? ✓ (No)
     Has your business taken advantage of market potential? ✓
     Has the competition been analyzed? ✓

  C. Personal selling
     Are your sales practices satisfactory? ✓

  D. Customer service
     Is customer service a priority? ✓
     Is there a rational balance between serving your customers' needs and good business practice? ✓ (most of the time)

  E. Advertising and public relations
     Do you select media for measurable results? ✓ (not always)
     Is your advertising consistent? ✓ (only in the Yellow Pages)
     Does your advertising budget make sense in terms of the level of business and its anticipated, planned growth? ✓

  F. Sales management
     Are salespersons and outside agents properly directed in their duties? ✓
     Do you establish individual sales goals? ✓
     Do you provide adequate sales support? ✓ (No)
     Are your salespersons trained? ✓ (No)

  G. Market planning
     Do you have a marketing budget? ✓ (No)
     Do you have a market plan? ✓ (in progress)
     Has your business taken advantage of market opportunities? ✓

II. Business Operations
  A. Purchasing
     Are reputable, competitive vendors used? NA
     Do you have a purchasing program? NA

continued on next page

Figure 6.1
Management Audit *continued from previous page*

	Yes	No

B. Inventory control
   Do you know what your inventory turnover is?
   Is slow-moving stock managed?   *NA*
   Have you established rational reordering policies?

C. Scheduling
   Do goods and materials move through the business without
      tie-ups and problems?   ✓ *(usually)*
   Do you know how long each job should take?   ✓

D. Quality control
   Are inferior incoming materials returned to vendors?
   Are reject rates minimized?
   Do you have a "do-it-right-the-first-time" policy?   ✓

E. Business growth
   Has your business grown at least above the rate of inflation?   ✓
   Have you met your asset growth, sales, and profit goals?   *✱ We didn't have goals — we need them!*

F. Site location
   Do you have the right business location?   ✓

G. Insurance
   Do you have an annual insurance review?   ✓ (No)
   Are the proper risks to your business (and to yourself) covered?   ✓ (No)
   Do you put your insurance package out to bid every year?   ✓ (No)

III. Financial
A. Bookkeeping and accounting
   Are your books adequate?   ✓
   Are records easy to come by?   ✓
   Can you get information when you need it?   ✓
   Do you have monthly Profit and Loss (Income) Statements?   ✓
   Do you have annual financial statements?   ✓

B. Budgeting
   Do you use a cash flow budget?   ✓
   Do you use deviation analysis monthly?   ✓
   Are capital equipment purchases budgeted?   ✓

C. Cost control
   Are cost items managed?   ✓
   Are high cost items treated separately?
   Is the budget used as the primary cost control tool?   ✓ (No)

D. Raising money
   Have you been successful in raising capital when it was needed?   ✓

continued on next page

Figure 6.1
Management Audit *continued from previous page*

	Yes	No
E. Credit and collection		
Do you know your C&C costs?		✓
Is your current policy successful?	✓	
Do you review C&C policies regularly?	✓	
Do you have a receivables management policy?	✓	
F. Dealing with banks		
Is your relationship with your lead banker open and friendly?	✓	
Do you have access to more than one source of financing?	✓	
G. Cost of money		
Do you compare the cost of money (interest, points) with your profit ratios?	✓	
Are interest rates and loan conditions appropriate?	✓	
H. Specific tools		
Do you know and use:		
1) Break-even analysis?	✓	
2) Cash flow projections and analysis?	✓	
3) Monthly Profit and Loss (Income) Statements?	✓	
4) Balance sheets?	✓	
5) Ratio analysis?	✓	
6) Industry operating ratios?	✓	
7) Tax planning?	✓	
IV. Personnel		
A. Hiring		
Has the right mix of people been hired?		✓
Do you hire from a pool of qualified applicants?	✓	
Do you maintain a file of qualified applicants?	✓	
B. Training		
Are your employees suitably trained for their jobs?	✓	
C. Motivating		
Do your employees appear to enjoy what they are doing?	✓ (not all the time)	
D. Enforcing policies		
Does there seem to be logic and order to what goes on in the business?	✓	
Are reviews and evaluations performed on schedule?		✓
E. Communicating		
Are people informed and brought in on decisions?	✓	
Do you create opportunities for employees to set their own goals?	✓	

continued on next page

Figure 6.1
Management Audit *continued from previous page*

	Yes	No

V. Administrative Management
A. Record keeping
   - Are records of past transactions and events easy to find? ✓
   - Are records retained for at least the minimum legal time period? ✓
   - Is access to personnel files limited? ✓ (No)

B. Problem solving
   - Are there few unresolved problems? ✓

C. Decision making
   - Are you decisive? ✓
   - Is there a chain of command? ✓

D. Government regulations
   - Are you aware of local, state, and federal regulations that affect your business? ✓

E. Leadership
   - Do you actually take charge of the business and its employees? ✓

F. Developing subordinates
   - If you were to die or suddenly become disabled, is there a ready successor? ✓

G. Business law
   - Do you have a working knowledge of applicable business law regarding contracts, agency, Uniform Commercial Code, and so on? ✓
   - Do you know how current contracts and other legal obligations affect your business? ✓

H. Dealing with professionals
   - Do you have and use an accountant, attorney, and business consultant? ✓
   - Do you use outside advisors? ✓

Figure 6.2
Good Management Scorecard

		Yes	No
I.	We operate with a complete and up-to-date business plan which includes:		
	A. One-year and three-year projections		✓
	B. A capital budget		✓
II.	We operate with an annual marketing plan which includes:		
	A. Specific sales and profit goals, and timetables	✓	
	B. Strategies and tactics for the next three years		✓
	C. Budgets, forecasts, and benchmarks	✓	
	D. A sales plan	✓	
	Our marketing plan also includes:		
	E. The demographics of our target markets		✓
	F. A thoughtful definition of the markets we serve	✓	
	G. A definition of the needs/wants our products and services fill	✓	
	H. An analysis of the growth potential of our markets	✓	
	I. A competitive analysis		✓
	J. A definition of our "Unique Selling Proposition"		✓
	K. Projections for other products or services that could be developed	✓	
	L. Timetables for research and development		✓
III.	We use monthly budgets and statements which include:		
	A. Thorough and up-to-date records	✓	
	B. Cash flow budget	✓	
	C. Profit and Loss (Income) Statement	✓	
	D. Balance sheet	✓	
	E. Deviation analysis	✓	
	F. Ratio analysis	✓	
	G. Standard cost comparisons		✓
	H. Cash reconciliation	✓	
IV.	We have developed an information base that allows us to:		
	A. Keep track of new developments in the industry	✓	
	B. Obtain and study key trade information	✓	
	C. Understand what "state of the art" means in this business		✓
	D. Provide customers with the best available information pertaining to our products and services	✓	
	E. Keep all our employees adequately informed	✓	
V.	I'm certain that the business is properly capitalized since I:		
	A. Base capitalization on worst-case planning		✓
	B. Have emergency funds (or access to them)		✓
	C. Have discussed this with my banker		✓
VI.	I understand the value of the business because I've made use of:		
	A. Professional appraisers		✓
	B. Present-value methods to evaluate terms		✓
	C. Professional tax planning counsel		✓
	D. Accurate, timely financial information	✓	

continued on next page

Figure 6.2
Good Management Scorecard *continued from previous page*

	Yes	No
VII. We strive to improve production, quality, and operations by:		
A. Keeping the plant in top condition		✓
B. Maintaining safe conditions	✓	
C. Establishing high standards	✓	
D. Standing behind our products/services	✓	
E. Not tolerating shoddy performance	✓	
F. Working for consistency	✓	
G. Using our company's "look" as a statement to our markets	✓	
VIII. Our personnel decisions are based on humane, carefully considered policies which include:		
A. Checklists to make sure objectives are clear		✓
B. Communication to make sure objectives are understood		✓
C. Written job descriptions		✓
D. Regular progress and performance evaluations	✓	
E. Fair hiring practices	✓	
F. Fair wage scales	✓	
IX. As for my own managerial skills, I work hard to:		
A. Develop my problem-solving abilities	✓	
B. Always stay calm		✓
C. Be objective		✓
D. Avoid investments in my own ego	✓	
E. Listen to my employees	✓	
F. Plan changes in our course to minimize negative effects	✓	
G. Make decisions promptly	✓	
H. Always get the facts behind problems		✓
I. Accept my own limitations	✓	
J. Delegate tasks that can be done more efficiently by someone else		✓
K. Analyze all available options		✓
L. Develop my reading/study habits	✓	
M. Improve my skills	✓	
N. Consider and evaluate risks	✓	
O. Be positive with customers, employees, and associates	✓	

Once more, "no" answers are red flags. "Yes" answers indicate acceptable levels, but may offer ideas for improved performance.

The next step is to relate your findings directly to your marketing plans. "No" answers to any item in Figure 6.1 or 6.2 are weaknesses that have to be acknowledged and dealt with. Those "yes" answers that identify areas of particular strength should also be noted; they are strengths to build on.

Your search for strengths and weaknesses goes further. Some areas of strength or weakness are outside your business. Others are internal, but are not captured in the checklists above.

If you can predict external weaknesses, you gain a major competitive advantage over the unprepared competitor.

Question 22: What is your business strong at?
Advantages may be things like a great product, skilled personnel, super location, close relationship with an ad agency, or outstanding technology. You want to find as many of these as possible to help you more sharply define your marketing niche.

External strengths include a number of factors you have little control over. For instance, your competition may be feeble, or your market expanding, or the local economy booming. These advantages tend to be temporary: No economy booms forever, markets have limits, and weak competition opens the doors for stronger competitors. Still, you want to be aware of and carefully monitor external advantages so you can benefit from them.

Question 23: What is your business weak at?
Samples of internal weaknesses include ineffective, untrained, or underutilized personnel, lack of sales support materials, frequent stockouts, poor quality, and undercapitalization. While some of these may have to be addressed from a company-wide point of view, some are essentially marketing problems. Do you have a marketing budget? If not, why not? Do you have sales training? If not, why not? Are sales support systems weak? Then strengthen them.

Your awareness and understanding of external problems and weaknesses help you handle them. Maybe you face new, aggressive competition, or the local economy is taking a nosedive, or your market is evaporating due to a new technology. You have to know what these larger forces are and how your business might respond to them. Maybe you can't control them, but you can control how your business reacts. If you can predict external weaknesses, you gain a major competitive advantage over the unprepared competitor. He or she gets swamped while you ride the wave.

List the strengths and weaknesses, both internal and external, that come to mind on Figure 6.3. Add those discovered in Figures 6.1 and 6.2. Then go out and look for more. This is an open-ended process which will become second nature. As you identify the strengths and weaknesses, ask yourself:
1. Can I change this circumstance?
2. Can I take advantage of or build on this?
3. If it is beyond my control, how does it or will it affect my business?
4. How long will these advantages and disadvantages last—and how can my business take advantage of these circumstances?

Figure 6.3
Strengths and Weaknesses

By: _RM & OL_   Date: _2/19/87_

List your business's strengths and weaknesses. Use Figures 6.1 and 6.2 as guides. Give very brief descriptions and categorize each as "internal" or "external" by checking the appropriate column.

	Internal	External
Strengths:		
1. Customer service	✓	
2. Financial management		
3. Bank relations		✓
4. Quality of service	✓	
5.		
Weaknesses:		
1. Advertising & PR	✓	
2. Market planning	✓	
3. Pricing	maybe!	
4. Insurance	✓	
5. Capitalization	✓	

The final step in this process is to review Figure 6.3 and rank the strengths and weaknesses. Since they represent significant opportunities and problems, you want to work on the most important first.

Figure 6.4
Analysis of a Specific Strength or Weakness

Fill out one of these forms for each strength or weakness.

By: _Al_ Date: _2/20/87_

Describe the strength or weakness. Be as factual as possible.

Customer service is a strength. We provide tax news and other information in our newsletter. We always meet deadlines and are always accessible — not just from 9 to 5.

What are the probable results of this strength or weakness?

We have loyal clients and close customer relations.

What should I do to capitalize on or correct this?

Promote word-of-mouth PR in our ads. Also use endorsements. Perhaps we should use this approach to get our clients' help: "We have a problem and we need your help."

Set dates for implementation and review.

Within a month: We will talk to 5 clients and aim to get 20 referrals.

Summary for Chapter Six
1. Two management audits have been conducted (Figures 6.1 and 6.2) to discover internal strengths and weaknesses. After reviewing them, the more important strengths and weaknesses have been listed on Figure 6.3.
2. Other strengths and weaknesses have been considered, and added to Figure 6.3.
3. These were then ranked in order of importance, and some of them were singled out for immediate attention using Figure 6.4.
4. Strengths and weaknesses help you or hinder you according to your awareness of them. If you are not reaching your sales and marketing goals, or if you think the goals should be higher, review this chapter.

Chapter Seven:
Advertising and Promotion

Figure 7.1
Promotion Audit

By: _GL_   Date: _2/21/87_

Do you:	Yes	No
Know where new business is coming from?	✓	
Keep track of referrals and thank the sources?	✓	
Track advertising and direct mail responses?	✓ (we need to do more!)	
Spend advertising dollars in proportion to your product mix?		✓
Project a strong, consistent image in all materials, signage, stationery, and so forth?	✓ (needs to be stronger)	
Have a professionally designed logo?		✓
Sell benefits to customers in all promotional material?		✓
Know what has worked, what has not worked, and why?	✓	
Have a yearly advertising, public relations, and promotion plan?		✓
Involve your entire staff in the promotional process?	✓	
Advertise to your staff as well as to your markets?		✓ (not enough)
Have strong relationships with media people and advertising professionals in your community?		✓
Assign one person to make sure your plan is implemented?		✓
Have a professionally designed "facilities brochure" which explains what your business is?		✓
Follow up promotional efforts with one-on-one selling (if appropriate)?	✓	
Have professional window and point-of-purchase displays?		✓
Analyze your probable competition in connection with the direct and indirect sales promotional methods you plan to use?		✓

For any "no" answer, you have another reason to use a professional advertising/public relations/promotion agency.

Advertising and promotion can't replace ongoing sales efforts.

Advertising and promotion are not substitutes for selling. They can make prospects aware of you, make them receptive to your products and services, even stir them to call or write for more information. But they can't replace ongoing sales efforts.

You have already done most of the groundwork for your advertising campaigns and other promotions. Effective creativity is based on thorough knowledge of products, target markets, and competitive conditions. Your advertising agency has to know what your objectives are, what your budget is, and when you plan to run your campaign.

Figure 7.2
Advertising Base

A successful promotional campaign requires answers to these questions.

1. *Who?* Who are your customers and prospects? You have already segmented your markets, so you can describe whom the promotion is aimed at. See Figure 3.4.
2. *Why?* What are you trying to accomplish? Increase sales? Introduce a new product? Retain or increase market share? Create or maintain an image? See Question 25 in this chapter.
3. *When?* Timing in advertising is all-important. The best promotion will bomb if the timing is off.
4. *What?* What specific products or services are you trying to move? What is their unique selling proposition?
5. *Where?* What media would be best for your campaign?
6. *How?* Leave this one to your advertising agency. You have enough to do running your business. You have to review and approve the campaign.

The details—the "where" and "how"—are less important than getting your message out. Your ad agency will save a lot of time here, help you make the right choices, and meet the deadlines. Many good campaigns are sabotaged by well-intentioned business owners who know a lot about their business but little about advertising and promotion. Unfortunately, everyone thinks he or she is a good copywriter and art director. Nothing could be further from the truth.

Advertising and promotion have to be managed the same way you manage other parts of your business. You have to know what resources you can afford to commit to them (Question 24), know what you want to accomplish (Question 25), and form a coherent strategy that ties in with your broader business and marketing goals (Question 26).

To illustrate the complexity of the problem, look at the promotional methods in Figure 7.3. Your promotional mix will employ several of these, plus others that aren't listed.

text continued on page 68

Figure 7.3
Promotion Smorgasbord

Promotion encompasses a wide range of activities:

Paid Advertising
   Radio
   Television
   Print
     Newspapers
     Magazines
     "Shoppers" (free or classified ad magazines)
     ✓Yellow Pages
     Special directories (regional, seasonal, Chamber of Commerce)
     Trade or industry directories (e.g., Thomas' Register of Manufacturers)
     Cooperative or "co-op" ad support from your vendors
     Outdoor billboards

Direct mail
   Letters
   ✓Newsletters
   Sales or product/service announcements
   ✓Flyers
   Postcards
   "Special customer" offers
   Brochures
   Direct response
   Coupons
   Bill stuffers

Public relations
   News releases
   ✓Articles in magazines, journals, etc.   *We should do more of these!*
   Open houses
   ✓Speaking engagements
   ✓Interview shows
   Sponsorship of community events and activities
   ✓Seminars
   ✓Workshops
   ✓Service club membership and participation
   Other club memberships

Telemarketing
   Inquiry handling
   ✓Direct marketing by phone
   Service: customer complaints, follow-up, special offers

continued on next page

Figure 7.3
Promotion Smorgasbord *continued from previous page*

✓ One-on-one selling
    Presentation materials *We need these!*
    ✓ Personal letters
    ✓ Customized proposals
    ✓ Some telemarketing
    Sales personnel training *We need this, too.*

Sales promotions
    Discounts ✓ *½ hour free consultation*
    Loss leaders
    Coupons
    "Buy one, get one free"

Specialty advertising
    Matchbooks, keychains, and other novelties
    Calendars
    Datebooks

We could use coffee mugs with our name and phone number on them!

Facilities
    Site location and shared advertising
    Signage
    Window displays
    Point-of-purchase displays
    Fixtures and layout of store
    Lighting

Other types of promotion
    Flyers
    Posters
    Handouts
    Blimps and balloons
    Sandwich boards

Choosing the right promotional mix for your business calls for professional skills. Check with your advertising and/or public relations agency.

Figure 7.4
Promotion = Time + Money

Time must be set aside for:

Task	Persons Involved	Frequency
Long- and short-term market planning	Key staff	Annually
Strategic planning for promotions	Key staff Ad agency	Semiannually
Discussion of marketing and promotional objectives	All staff	Quarterly
Discussion and evaluation of specific promotional activities and materials	All staff	Before and after each campaign
Implementation and scheduling	You Ad agency	Monthly or as necessary

Other important time-intensive promotional efforts include development and production of materials, all public relations activities, development and purchase of mailing lists, coordination of bulk mailings, writing and mailing individual letters and proposals, telephone, mail, and personal follow-up of promotional efforts.

Money must be set aside for:

Public relations and general information materials
    Printing
    Photography
    Sponsorship of events
    Open houses
    Mailings
    Community service advertising
    Donations
    Memberships (Rotary, Chamber, etc.)

Targeted product and service campaigns
    Copywriting and design fees
    Media placement costs
    Photography, typesetting, and graphic design costs
    Printing
    Bulk mail (fulfillment)
    Mailing lists
    Studio and talent costs of radio/TV spot production
    Advertising agency fees other than for copy and design

Reducing advertising costs when business starts to slow down will only accelerate a sales slump, not save your profitability.

Incomplete campaigns just eat up money—see Figure 7.4. You might as well burn the cash and save the time; you'd come out ahead.

Question 24: What is your advertising and promotion budget?
If you don't have an advertising and promotion budget, you don't have a rational marketing plan.

Advertising and promotion is a cost of doing business. Rigorously and ruthlessly suppress the urge to cut it at the first sign of sluggish sales. Build it in, like payments on plant or equipment or any other fixed cost, and be prepared to increase it. An advertising campaign is like a military campaign. Attaining your objectives calls for careful allocation and concentration of your resources so you can successfully implement your strategy.

You buy and maintain market share with advertising as well as with product, service, distribution, and other business efforts. When sales are off, increase advertising efforts. When sales are up, you may be able to ease off a little—run ads less often, for example. Reducing advertising costs when business starts to slow down will only accelerate a sales slump, not save your profitability.

How do you set an advertising budget? There are four common methods:

1. *Percent of sales.* You can get trade figures to show how others in your industry allocate their advertising dollars. Figure this on your anticipated or desired sales, and treat advertising and promotion as a fixed expense. If sales levels or goals increase, change the advertising budget. Do not cut advertising budgets in response to short-term sales slumps.

This method is inflexible, and doesn't reflect the cost structures and marketing goals of your business. It does provide a good baseline. If you differ seriously from industry standards, have a good reason for that deviation and be prepared to justify that deviation to your banker.

2. *Flat dollar or "leftover" budget.* This is sometimes arrived at by adding all the other expenses and then allocating what's left to advertising. Another way: Take last year's advertising expenses and increase them a set percentage or amount.

This leaves your advertising unbudgeted, your campaigns incomplete, and your marketing efforts gutted. Flat dollar budgeting is far and away the most popular method for small business owners, which should provide a competitive opening for you to take advantage of.

3. *Project-by-project or whim budgeting.* While this approach may enrich your advertising agency, it is effectively no budget at all. It lets you reduce advertising without noticing that you are doing so. It does have great flexibility, which is a strength if used in conjunction with a budget for ongoing advertising and promotional efforts.

4. *Flexible budgeting.* Set a lower limit, based on experience, industry standards, and sales goals. Then be prepared to increase it, on a project basis, to take advantage of opportunities or to turn a sales slump around.

Smart small business owners use two budgets to support their promotional campaigns. The first is a percent of sales or flat dollar budget for ongoing advertising and promotional expenses, while the other is a discretionary budget (project budget) with well-defined applications and dollar limits.

Question 25: What are your advertising and promotion objectives?
If you reach your advertising objectives, you should be closer to attaining your marketing objectives. Advertising is tactical rather than strategic—see Figure 8.3: Strategies and Tactics on page 82 for a more detailed explanation. Your advertising goals serve your marketing goals, not vice versa.

Figure 7.5
Advertising/Promotion Goals

These are goals some astute small business owners have set for their advertising and promotional campaigns. They are intended to nudge your thinking, not as a comprehensive list of goals.

Do you want to:
1. Penetrate specialized markets? Which ones? What are the measures of progress (unit sales, dollar sales, other benchmarks)?
2. Sell more to present customers? How?
3. Specialize in terms of product or services? Which ones? Why?
4. Change your business's image? Why? To what? How?
5. Penetrate geographical markets more deeply? Which areas? How?
6. Create "top-of-mind" awareness? How?
7. Expand demographically? To whom? What market segments?
8. Increase sales of specific products or services? How?
9. Announce a new product/service, new product/service mix, or new location?
10. Support community projects for public relations benefits?

Use the answers to these questions to help decide how you want to be perceived, whom you plan to do business with, and what you want to sell.

Question 26: How do you promote your business?
If you insist on doing your own publicity, promotion, and advertising, ask yourself once more: What business am I in? If it isn't self-promotion, then you'd do better to rely on outside advisors to help you set and implement your advertising and promotional policies. This is a specialized field, and too important an area for amateur efforts.

If you insist on doing your own publicity, promotion, and advertising, ask yourself once more: What business am I in?

Figure 7.6
Initial Advertising Agenda

When you work with an advertising agent or public relations expert, the first item on their agenda will be to determine:
1. What business are you in?
2. What do you want to accomplish with your advertising, publicity, or promotion?
3. What do you sell?
4. To whom?
5. What are your sales and marketing goals?
6. What's your budget?
7. What's your timetable for achieving your goals?

You can simplify much of the groundwork that effective advertising and promotion require. In fact, most of the work can and should be done by you. After all, it's your vision and experience and intuition that make your business special.

If these seem to be familiar questions, they are. Advertising and promotional campaigns begin with your current situation, rely on the budgetary guidelines to help you reach your goals, and absolutely demand thorough knowledge of what your business is now and will become. And as you've seen by now, these are time-consuming questions to answer. Quick answers just aren't enough. You need facts, documentation, analysis, and more facts. The questions in Figure 7.7 will help focus your preliminary efforts.

An advertising plan (including promotional efforts) involves eight steps. Now that you know your advertising/promotional budget and your objectives, you can set down a preliminary plan fairly quickly.

1. *Identify long-term objectives.* These are ultimate goals, probably a year or more out. As always, make them as precise as you can: dollar or unit sales, time frames, persons responsible for attaining them, some indication of the resources you can allocate to achieving them.

2. *Define short-term goals and priorities.* What do you want to get done next month, next week, tomorrow?

3. *Assemble resources.* Have your in-house information available. A sketch of your options and priorities is helpful. Have your business plan near to hand.

4. *Select an advertising agency* to guide you through the thickets of media selection and production scheduling. See Figure 7.8.

5. *Schedule projects.* This is the heart of your advertising plan, and calls for a large calendar to help establish timelines. (Figure 7.9 gives you an idea of how much time is involved at each stage of production.) For each advertisement or project, ask:
    A. Where will it run?
    B. What is the "street date" when it will appear?
    C. What size will it be?
    D. How much will it cost to prepare?
    E. What is the media cost?

Important considerations to keep in mind throughout the plan are timing, repetition (you get bored with the ad before your prospects and customers are aware that it's running), and reinforcement. Ads alone don't sell—but they create awareness and support your other selling efforts. You must spell out deadlines and assign responsibility to one individual (perhaps yourself) to make the most of your budget.

Ads alone don't sell—but they create awareness and support your other selling efforts.

6. *Choose media.* See Figure 7.10.

7. *Specs for ads.* Usually you leave this to your agency, but if you do it yourself, be sure to include:
    A. Purpose of the ad: What do you want to accomplish?
    B. Preferred approach: Hard sell? Soft sell? Humor? Fit the approach to your image.
    C. Size and frequency of ad.
    D. A creative budget.
    E. Deadlines.

8. *Evaluate the results.* Unevaluated advertising might give you some short-run advantages, but if you can learn from your advertising and promotional experiences, your advertising can become more effective.

You can test many elements of your advertising by following traditional methods. These work; they have been well proven.
    A. Offer coupons.
    B. Offer sales of certain items.
    C. Split runs of your ad. (For example, run your ad in a national magazine only to certain geographic areas.)
    D. Track inquiries. (For example, ask people to "write Department XYZ" for more information.)
    E. Look for patterns of response (timing, number, percentages).
    F. Keep a scrapbook of your ads and other efforts. Keep one for your competitors, too.
    G. Ask your staff what they think of the ads.
    H. Ask customers what they read and watch. See Figure 7.11: Ten-Second Media Quiz.

Summary for Chapter Seven
1. You completed a promotion audit (Figure 7.1) to determine where you need professional advertising help.
2. You looked at different ways of promoting your business (Figure 7.3) and what goes into planning a promotional campaign (Figure 7.4). Then you need to set goals and an advertising budget.
3. Figure 7.8 will help you evaluate ad agencies and choose the one most likely to help you reach your advertising and promotion goals. Figures 7.6 and 7.7 will help you set an agenda with your ad agency.
4. Work with your ad agency to develop an advertising action plan. Set a timetable for the objectives you want to reach, when actions will be taken to implement these objectives, and how much money will be needed at specific times to achieve your objectives.

Figure 7.7
Advertising/Promotional Questions

Ask and answer these questions:
1. Markets:
    What is your market mix?
    What percentage of your business comes from:
        Individuals? *15%*
        Small businesses? *75%*
        Big businesses? *10%*
        Local trade? *80%*
        Regional trade? *20%*
        National or international trade?
    What is the market potential?

2. Products/Services:
    Are they:
        Innovative? ✓
        Specialized?
        Diversified? ✓ *May be too diversified — a problem!*
        Commodity?
        Packaged?
        Tailor-made or customized? ✓
    (Answer "how" to each "yes" answer.)

3. Image:
    Would you describe your business as:
        Formal?
        Informal? ✓
        With a community focus? *} we can't decide*
        With a regional or national focus?
        Aggressive?
        Relaxed or laid-back? *} 50/50*
        Sophisticated?

continued on next page

Figure 7.7
Advertising/Promotional Questions *continued from previous page*

    "Down-home"?
    Specialized?
    General in outlook?
Does this description fit the way you want to be perceived as well as the way you see yourself now? Or do you want to change your company's image? *We need to create one!*

4. Business strengths:
    What special expertise or experience do you have?
    Does your business offer:
        Longevity in the community?
        Convenient location?
        Outstanding service reputation? ✓
        Other benefits? (specify)

5. Competition:
    How do you stack up against your competition's:
        Market share?
        Image? *Low penetration*

6. Customer base:
    Do you sell:
        Many products and services to a few loyal customers? ✓
        Several products to a narrowly defined industry?
        Single products to a diverse client base? ✓

    Do you have a data base to tell you:
        The product mix for each customer? ✓
        Where their business came from? (referral, advertising, etc.) ✓
        The basic demographics of your markets? *We should get one!*

Figure 7.8
Selecting a Promotional Pro

When shopping for an advertising or public relations agency, ask:

1. *What process does your agency use in analyzing client needs?*
A successful program includes as much or more planning as execution. You want to be sure that the agency has the "mental horsepower" to see beyond the obvious and move your promotional programs beyond the limits of your own abilities.

2. *Once you've determined my needs, how will you position my company?*
The agency has to be your partner in developing a creative strategy for your business. What process do they use to develop your communications goals? Why?

continued on next page

Figure 7.8
Selecting a Promotional Pro *continued from previous page*

3. *How do you measure the effectiveness of your strategies?*
Results can be measured in attitude changes, exposure, awareness, sales increases, specific information requested—and other ways. Make sure you are comfortable with their measurement plans, and that you understand why those are valid measurements. Be very leery of "You can't measure the results, but..." excuses. If it can't be measured, you can't afford it.

4. *How do you keep us informed about your activities?*
You should get tear sheets, comprehensive and understandable billing, and full explanations of what is going on when you request it. The smoke and mirror approach is fine for movies, but not for your investment.

5. *Who else have you worked with, especially firms like mine? What success (and horror) stories do you have? Whom may we contact?*
Customers, both happy and unhappy, provide the least biased information about how well performance matched expectations.

6. *Describe a successful program for a business like ours. What were the goals of the program? What strategies and tactics did you use? How did you measure your success?*
You want to separate fact from selling. Ask for names and numbers.

7. *If the campaign is public relations (unpaid advertising), what are your relationships with the media? Are you on a first-name basis with "influencers" in our field?*
Nothing is as helpful as a personal friend in high places. PR firms work to establish these relationships, and are (usually) proud of them.

8. *How do you approach creativity? How do you measure it? How do you involve clients in the creative process?*
The aim is to find out if they value creativity as a tool (good) or as an end in itself (bad). This is a judgment call you have to make—once again, smoke and mirrors are fine for entertainment, but not for your money.

9. *What important clients have you lost in the past year? Why did you lose them? May I speak with them?*
An agency that badmouths a former client will eventually badmouth you. Every agency loses clients to their competition; good agents know why and aren't ashamed or antagonistic about it.

10. *Most important of all: Who will be working on our account day-by-day?*
You want to have experienced talent working for you, not the newest hire. You can't afford to train beginners. Make sure the agency's top talent is working for you.

Figure 7.9
Production Timelines

	Print Ad	Two-Color Brochure	Coupon	Letter/ Press Release
Choose publication	1-7 days	Not Applicable	Not Applicable	1-3 days
Assign tasks/ hire professionals	1-2 days	1-2 days	1-2 days	1 day
Write	1-4 days	1-7 days	1-2 days	1-3 days
Edit	1-2 days	1-3 days	1 day	1-2 days
Design	1-4 days	1-7 days	1-2 days	1-2 days*
Get estimates for printing/ choose printer	Not Applicable	1-3 days	1-2 days	1 day
Photography	2-7 days*	2-7 days*	Not Applicable	2-7 days*
Illustration	2-7 days*	2-7 days*	Not Applicable	Not Applicable
Paste-up	2-4 days	2-7 days	1-2 days	1-2 days*
Printing/ proofing	Not Applicable	1-3 weeks	1-3 days	1-3 days
Total time	**1-4 weeks**	**2-6 weeks**	**1-2 weeks**	**1-2 weeks**

* If Necessary

Figure 7.10
Media Advantages and Disadvantages at a Glance

	Advantages	Disadvantages
Newspapers	• Your ad has size and shape, and can be as large as necessary to communicate as much of a story as you care to tell. • The distribution of your message can be limited to your geographic area. • Split-run tests are available to test your copy and your offer. • Free help is usually available to create and produce your ad. • Fast closings. The ad you decide to run today can be in your customer's hands two days from now.	• Clutter—your ad has to compete for attention against large ads run by supermarkets and department stores. • Poor photo reproduction limits creativity. • A price-oriented medium—most ads are for sales. • Short shelf life. The day after a newspaper appears, it's history. • Waste circulation. You're paying to send your message to a lot of people who will probably never be in the market to buy from you. • A highly visible medium. Your competitors can quickly react to your prices.
Magazines	• High reader involvement means more attention will be paid to your advertisement. • Less waste circulation. You can place your ads in magazines read primarily by buyers of your product or service. • Better quality paper permits better photo reproduction and full color ads. • The smaller page (generally 8-1/2 by 11 inches) permits even small ads to stand out.	• Long lead times (generally 90 days) mean you have to make plans a long time in advance. • Higher space costs plus higher creative costs.
Yellow Pages	• Everyone uses the Yellow Pages. • Ads are reasonably inexpensive. • You can easily track responses.	• All of your competitors are listed, so you run the ad as a defensive measure. • Ads are not very creative, since they follow certain formats.
Radio	• A universal medium—enjoyed at home, at work, and while driving. Most people listen to the radio at one time or another during the day. • Permits you to target your advertising dollars to the market most likely to respond to your offer. • Permits you to create a personality for your business using only sounds and voices. • Free creative help is usually available. • Rates can generally be negotiated. • Least inflated medium. During the past ten years, radio rates have gone up less than other media.	• Because radio listeners are spread over many stations, to totally saturate your market you have to advertise simultaneously on many stations. • Listeners cannot refer back to your ads to go over important points. • Ads are an interruption to the entertainment. Because of this, radio ads must be repeated to break through the listener's "tune-out" factor. • Radio is a background medium. Most listeners are doing something else while listening, which means your ad has to work hard to be listened to and understood. • Advertising costs are based on ratings which are approximations based on diaries kept in a relatively small fraction of a region's homes.

continued on next page

Figure 7.10
Media Advantages and Disadvantages at a Glance *continued from previous page*

	Advantages	Disadvantages
Television	• Permits you to reach great numbers of people on a national or regional level. • Independent stations and cable offer new opportunities to pinpoint local audiences. • Very much an image-building medium.	• Ads on network affiliates are concentrated in local news broadcasts and on station breaks. • Creative and production costs can quickly mount up. • Preferred items are often sold out far in advance. • Most ads are ten or thirty seconds long, which limits the amount of information you can communicate.
Direct Mail	• Your advertising message is targeted to those most likely to buy your product or service. • Your message can be as long as necessary to fully tell your story. • You have total control over all elements of creation and production. • A "silent" medium. Your message is hidden from your competitors until it's too late for them to react.	• Long lead times required for creative printing and mailing. • Requires coordinating the services of many people: artists, photographers, printers, etc. • Each year over 20% of the population moves, meaning you must work hard to keep your mailing list up to date. • Likewise, a certain percentage of the names on a purchased mailing list is likely to be no longer useful.
Telemarketing	• You can easily answer questions about your product/service. • It's easy to prospect and find the right person to talk to. • Cost effective compared to direct sales. • Highly measurable results. • You can get a lot of information if your script is properly structured.	• Lots of businesses use telemarketing. • Professionals should draft the script and perform the telemarketing in order for it to be effective. • Can be extremely expensive. • Most appropriate for high-ticket retail items or professional services.
Specialty Advertising (balloons, sandwich boards, key charms, etc.)	• Can be attention grabbers if they are done well. • Can give top-of-mind awareness. • Gets your name in front of people.	• Difficult to target your market. • Can be an inappropriate medium for some businesses. • It's difficult to find items that are appropriate for certain businesses.

Figure 7.11
Ten-Second Media Quiz *This really doesn't apply to us*

Please list the newspapers you read regularly.

	Daily	Weekly
1. First choice	_____	_____
2. Second choice	_____	_____
3. Third choice	_____	_____

Please list the radio stations you listen to regularly.

1. First choice _____

2. Second choice _____

3. Third choice _____

4. Fourth choice _____

5. Fifth choice _____

Have you recently seen or heard our advertising?

Where? _____

Thank you for your help!

Your Logo

Chapter Eight:
Strategic Marketing

"It is not enough to be industrious; so are the ants. What are you industrious about?" —Henry David Thoreau

All marketing decisions are strategic.

Strategic marketing takes account of the competitive nature of business and keeps your efforts focused. All of the preceding chapters have implicitly taken a strategic bent; now you want to make your own strategy explicit.

Why consciously choose a marketing strategy? Your marketing efforts are goal-directed, and you want to be sure that the goals you are aiming at are the goals you wish to reach. Strategic planning makes sure that you do the right things. Your marketing plan helps you do those things right.

Question 27: What marketing problems have you discovered so far?
All businesses have problems. The strengths of your competition, your business' competitive weaknesses, technological changes, shifting public tastes—the list can go on and on.

Review Figures 1.6, 2.2, 2.5, 4.3, 4.4, 4.5, and all of Chapter Six, especially Figure 6.3.

Ask yourself (and your staff and other interested persons):
1. What marketing problems are we currently working on?
2. What problems are we avoiding?
3. What are we going to do about them?
4. Who is responsible for solving these problems—and when? With what resources?
5. Why haven't we reached our sales and/or marketing goals in the past?
6. What might keep us from reaching our current sales goals?

Question 28: How do you plan to solve these problems?
List several possible solutions to each major problem. Don't just pick the first solution that occurs to you. It probably isn't the best solution. The trick is to define the problem as factually as possible, then look for a number of possible causes. Facts and analysis will prevent you from finding a remedy for the symptom rather than the disease.

Then ask yourself how your strategies will affect or be affected by these problems.

If problems have to be resolved, assign responsibility for solving each problem to one person. Make sure to allow enough authority and sufficient resources to that person (you or someone else). Maybe the solution will involve brainstorming or other techniques. The important thing is to first recognize the problem, then carefully define and analyze it before taking action.

Strategic planning makes sure that you do the right things. Your marketing plan helps you do those things right.

Goals have to be clear, measurable, and most important of all, easy to communicate.

Figure 8.1
Problem Solving Worksheet

By: _OL_   Date: _2/24/87_

1. What is the problem? Cite standard and deviation from standard if available.

   We lack a single focus.

2. Possible causes: *We've always taken all business which comes our way, and we haven't established a niche for ourselves.*

3. Interim solution:
   ① *Define short-term market goal: Go after auto market*
   ② *Do profitability study to determine where time gets billed and where time is wasted.*

Question 29: Are the goals stated in Chapter One still valid? If not, what are your new goals?
Return to Figures 1.3 and 1.5.

Preliminary goal setting is a starting point, not your final decision. Revise your sales and marketing goals in light of the analysis in the preceding chapters. Maybe the strategies that make the best sense for your business call for a revision of your goals.

If you do change some of your goals, what are the new ones? Collect them on Figure 8.2. Be as specific as you can. For example:
   For next year:
   1. Increase sales of Product A 15% by December;
   2. Lower reject rate 5% in the next quarter;
   3. Open branch office in St. Paul in six months, with sales goals and budgets established by Harvey and approved by Maude due on my desk no later than September 15th.

And so forth. Goals have to be clear, measurable, and most important of all, easy to communicate. Your marketing strategies and plan are built to accomplish these goals—and people have to know what the goals are. Fuzzy goals such as "Increase sales" or "Cut the reject rate" or "Get that dratted branch going" are seriously deficient, don't provide the timetables or assign responsibilities, and as a result are not effective.

Figure 8.2
Personal and Business Goal Summary

Personal goals include non-financial goals as well as financial goals. Limit the goals to the most important.

1. List your personal goals:
   A. Improve health and increase level of energy.
   B. Change the mix of work I'm currently doing.
   C. Make more time to enjoy life.
   D. Make more money.
   E.

2. List your business goals:

	For next year:	In three years:
Quantitative Goals:		
A. Sales ($)	$175,000	$265,000
B. Sales (unit)		
C. Profit ($)	$50,000	$100,000 (at least!)
D. Profit (% sales)		
E. Market share ← *Needs work*		
F. Company net worth ($)		
G. Number of employees	5	8
Qualitative Goals:		
A. Market position	Small business experts	More niche oriented
B. Kind of business	Accounting	More business consulting
C. Target markets	Auto businesses	Consulting companies
D. Business culture or style	Some	Even more professional!
E. Other (specify):	Improve use of time	

3. Potential conflicts between personal and business goals:
   We need to work out a marketing plan so our business goals reflect our personal goals. We'll need to add personnel if we are to grow.

4. Comments:

Question 30: How do you plan to achieve these goals?
That's what your marketing plan is all about. Each goal calls for a series of actions. The strategies in Figure 8.4 set broad marketing objectives; the more specific goals in Figure 8.2 define the tactical boundaries. You won't attain your goals all at once, but rather in stages.

If you have chosen your strategies wisely and made sure that reaching the goals of Figure 8.2 lead to attaining the strategic objectives, the steps should be clear. As with any other tactical plan, you have to know what the goal is, when it is to be reached, what you have by way of resources to attain that goal, and what the possible barriers are. Some of these details will be spelled out in chapter ten, "The Sales Plan." Others will be treated in the marketing plan itself.

Figure 8.3
Strategies and Tactics

All strategic elements must be defined in terms of needs, attitudes, and unmet desires in the market. These will include known needs that can be accurately determined by investigations and hypothetical needs that must be nourished to become a market need.

Tactics are:	Strategies are:
Concrete	Conceptual
Specific	General
Individual	Complex
Linear	Organic
Sequential	Interactive and systemic

Strategic planning must define goals that are qualitative in nature. These qualitative goals include:

Positioning: What is the position of your organization in its target markets and among your competitors? How is it viewed by the market?
Segmentation: What are the demographics, attitudes, and tastes of your defined target markets?
Cultural: What is the culture of your business?
Stylistic: What is the style of your business?
Differentiation: In what ways does your business and its product/service structure differ from all other organizations offering similar products/services?
Functional: What purpose does the organization and its product/service structure fulfill beyond its own parochial needs?

Quantitative elements to be defined include: price strategy, market share, growth rate, cost characteristics, sales and profit goals, production and distribution goals, and logistics.

Selecting a marketing strategy is a four-step process:

1. Examine past and current marketing strategies. Have yours been "business as usual," "get whatever pieces of business we can," or "follow-the-leader"? These are the three most common and least effective strategies for small business owners. Few small business owners plan to run their businesses in these ways, but inattention and habit make these choices inevitable.

You can't change strategies overnight. They are built into the culture of your business. Your goals and methods of achieving those goals (including business practices and relationships of people within the business) are inextricably mixed up with your strategic choices. The strategies and culture evolve together slowly; they change slowly, too.

Your strategies should reflect your attitudes and personality. Strategies can be active or reactive, aggressive or defensive, risk-inclined or risk-averse. If your own style is relaxed and risk-averse, an aggressive, high-risk strategy probably won't work. If you enjoy risk and being ahead of the crowd, then a defensive, reactive strategy will drive you up the wall. That doesn't mean that you can't adopt a conflicting strategy for a short while—but if you adopt one counter to your feelings, be aware of the potential conflict.

In Figure 8.4: Checklist for Strategic Planning, check the strategies that best fit your business's past and present practices. While the list is not exhaustive, it encompasses most strategies that small business owners can realistically apply. Don't try to pick the best strategies for your business yet. You have a few steps still to take.

2. Summarize personal and business objectives. Include your personal goals in your marketing plans. If you want to retire in five years, fine. Plan for it. If you want to work until you drop, fine. Plan for it. If you want your business to remain small enough so you can bring your dog to work, great. It can be done. Just don't set up your business to thwart yourself. If you want to see how big a business you can build, go ahead. But don't do it unless it makes sense to you, personally.

In Figure 1.3 you set down preliminary personal goals. Review them now. In Figure 1.5 you listed preliminary business goals. Review them also. If your personal priorities aren't in line with your business priorities, change your business priorities. You have better things to do with your life than warp it for the benefit of your business. Review Figure 8.2. Figure 8.5 should include all changes and revisions of your goals to date; it will be the basis of your marketing plan.

3. Now return to Figure 8.4. Examine each of these strategies and ask yourself if, given your resources and competitive situation, each would help you reach your goals. You will probably want to use more than one strategy, or modify one or more to better fit your business.

4. Choose the simplest strategies for your business. To be effective, strategies have to be communicated. Fancy strategies look great on paper, but if they

text continued on page 87

Your strategies should reflect your attitudes and personality.

Figure 8.5
Personal and Business Goal Summary

Let's think about this some more and review it next week!

1. List your personal goals.
   A.
   B.
   C.
   D.
   E.

2. List your business goals.

   Quantitative Goals: For next year: In three years:
   A. Sales ($)
   B. Sales (unit)
   C. Profit ($)
   D. Profit (% sales)
   E. Market share
   F. Company net worth ($)
   G. Number of employees

   Qualitative Goals:
   A. Market position
   B. Kind of business
   C. Target markets
   D. Business culture or style
   E. Other (specify):
   _____
   _____

3. Potential conflicts between personal and business goals:

4. Comments:

Selecting a marketing strategy is a four-step process:

1. Examine past and current marketing strategies. Have yours been "business as usual," "get whatever pieces of business we can," or "follow-the-leader"? These are the three most common and least effective strategies for small business owners. Few small business owners plan to run their businesses in these ways, but inattention and habit make these choices inevitable.

You can't change strategies overnight. They are built into the culture of your business. Your goals and methods of achieving those goals (including business practices and relationships of people within the business) are inextricably mixed up with your strategic choices. The strategies and culture evolve together slowly; they change slowly, too.

Your strategies should reflect your attitudes and personality. Strategies can be active or reactive, aggressive or defensive, risk-inclined or risk-averse. If your own style is relaxed and risk-averse, an aggressive, high-risk strategy probably won't work. If you enjoy risk and being ahead of the crowd, then a defensive, reactive strategy will drive you up the wall. That doesn't mean that you can't adopt a conflicting strategy for a short while—but if you adopt one counter to your feelings, be aware of the potential conflict.

In Figure 8.4: Checklist for Strategic Planning, check the strategies that best fit your business's past and present practices. While the list is not exhaustive, it encompasses most strategies that small business owners can realistically apply. Don't try to pick the best strategies for your business yet. You have a few steps still to take.

2. Summarize personal and business objectives. Include your personal goals in your marketing plans. If you want to retire in five years, fine. Plan for it. If you want to work until you drop, fine. Plan for it. If you want your business to remain small enough so you can bring your dog to work, great. It can be done. Just don't set up your business to thwart yourself. If you want to see how big a business you can build, go ahead. But don't do it unless it makes sense to you, personally.

In Figure 1.3 you set down preliminary personal goals. Review them now. In Figure 1.5 you listed preliminary business goals. Review them also. If your personal priorities aren't in line with your business priorities, change your business priorities. You have better things to do with your life than warp it for the benefit of your business. Review Figure 8.2. Figure 8.5 should include all changes and revisions of your goals to date; it will be the basis of your marketing plan.

3. Now return to Figure 8.4. Examine each of these strategies and ask yourself if, given your resources and competitive situation, each would help you reach your goals. You will probably want to use more than one strategy, or modify one or more to better fit your business.

4. Choose the simplest strategies for your business. To be effective, strategies have to be communicated. Fancy strategies look great on paper, but if they

Your strategies should reflect your attitudes and personality.

text continued on page 87

Figure 8.4
Checklist for Strategic Planning

This checklist presents a range of small business strategic options proven in hundreds of applications.

Past	Current	Future	Strategy	Probable Consequences, Risks
			Sample Marketing Strategies	
1.			Rationalize distribution. Cut back to most efficient network; look at volume, geography, type.	*Increase profit margins, lower inventories, some costs go down; may need new investment; moderate risk.*
2.			Develop the market. Create demand for a brand new product.	*Very high marketing costs, may increase receivables, impacts profit and loss statement, hinders cash flow; large expense budget; high risk—but high reward if successful.*
3.			Penetrate the market. Increase market share: lower price, broaden product line mix, add service and sales personnel, increase advertising.	*Increases marketing and sales expenses, need for working capital, and need for capital investment if capacity grows. Reduces short-term earnings; high risk.*
4.			Promote new products to present market. Develop, broaden, or replace products in product line, sell to present market.	*Lower unit costs; increase inventory, sales volume, profit and cash flow; some capital investment needed, increased development, design, and manufacturing costs; moderate to high risk.*
5.			Seek new markets, same products. Expand existing markets by geography (abroad) or type for existing products.	*Increase sales volume and profit margins as unit costs drop and as new market grows; higher short-term selling costs; modest capital investment, increased working capital; high risk.*
6.			Develop new products for new markets. Invest in developing, manufacturing, and marketing products unrelated to product line for new markets.	*Will increase sales volume, costs, profits (if successful); will have same problems as a new business if products unrelated to current line; will need more working capital, may need new capital investment; increase in sales and marketing costs; high risk.*
7.			Rationalize market. Prune back to most profitable segments, higher volume segments; concentrate marketing focus.	*Reduce sales volume, increase profit margins, lower working capital needs, increase cash flow as percent of sales, decrease receivables; willingness to accept lower sales totals; moderate risk.*
8.			Maintain products and market share. Business continues as before; same products, same markets.	*Increase at industry growth rate with stable, short-term profit margins; decrease working capital and increase cash throw off overtime; may lower unit costs; investment in strategies to hold position; low risk.*

continued on next page

Figure 8.4
Checklist for Strategic Planning (*continued from previous page.*)

Past	Current	Future	Strategy	Probable Consequences, Risks
			Sample Management Strategies	
9.			Cut costs. Reduce costs uniformly through management edicts.	*Increase profit margins, achieve lowest possible return of all efficiency strategies; needs excellent implementation to apply intelligently; moderate risks due to arbitrary nature of cutbacks—may have invidious consequences.*
10.			Abandon unit. Sell or liquidate unit because it doesn't fit in with company—or because it is worth more to someone else.	*Improve cash flow from sale of assets, create possible morale problem in rest of organization; low risk.*
			Sample Financial Strategies	
11.			Rationalize product line. Narrow profit line to most profitable items.	*Reduce sales volume, improve working capital, profitability, may lead to under-utilizing assets in short term; hard to give up old winners; low to moderate risk.*
12.			Pure survival. Hunker down to meet most adverse conditions by eliminating or paring down some aspects of the business.	*Reduce sales volume, considerably reduce costs, improve ROI short term, improve cash flow temporarily; courage needed, moderate risk due to possible loss of market share, some danger from creditors and other trade sources.*
13.			Pause in action. Slow down or establish a one-year moratorium on new capital investment; normal maintenance of business.	*No effect on sales short term, may disrupt growth plans, weaken business over long term, decrease sales and earnings if pause is too lengthy; courage and large measure of steadfastness; low risk.*
			Sample Production Strategies	
14.			Improve technology. Improve operating efficiency through technological improvements in physical plant, equipment, or processes.	*Decrease variable costs and increase fixed costs—an overall reduction can considerably increase profits, affects sales volume slightly; low to high capital investment; low to moderate risk depending on the extent to which the particular technology is proven.*
			Sample Operating Strategies	
15.			Improve methods and functions. Invest in new ways of doing existing tasks by adding new 'soft' technologies: e.g., new patterns of work flow, CAD/CAM, production planning, inventory control, etc., to improve effectiveness and/or efficiency.	*Improve operating performance, improve functional rather than product costs; expense investment; creative thinking needed; low to moderate risk.*

Figure 8.5
Personal and Business Goal Summary

Let's think about this some more and review it next week!

1. List your personal goals.
   A.
   B.
   C.
   D.
   E.

2. List your business goals.
   Quantitative Goals:　　　　　For next year:　　In three years:
   　A. Sales ($)
   　B. Sales (unit)
   　C. Profit ($)
   　D. Profit (% sales)
   　E. Market share
   　F. Company net worth ($)
   　G. Number of employees
   Qualitative Goals:
   　A. Market position
   　B. Kind of business
   　C. Target markets
   　D. Business culture or style
   　E. Other (specify):
   　_____
   　_____

3. Potential conflicts between personal and business goals:

4. Comments:

continued from page 83

present opportunities for misunderstanding, you can count on their being misunderstood. The simplest strategies are the best strategies.

Now make your final strategic choices.

    A. Test them for consistency with each other. You don't want to pursue contradictory strategies.

    B. Test them for feasibility. If they require more resources than you can muster, they won't work.

    C. Test them for coherence: Do they fit your business? Do they tend toward unifying the focus of your marketing efforts? Do they form an understandable, easily communicated grand strategy?

    D. Finally: Make sure that they are acceptable to your employees. If you can't generate company-wide support, the strategy will fail. This is where complicated strategies break down. If you can't communicate the strategies clearly, you have a problem. (This is a blessing in disguise. In competitive markets, your competition will look at your strategy and try to improve on it by making it a bit fancier here, a bit more complicated there. Let them be complex. You stay simple, and win the marketplace.)

Summary for Chapter Eight
1. Marketing problems (and problems that might affect your marketing plans) were listed and addressed in Figure 8.1.
2. Personal and business goals appear twice. Figure 8.2 is based on the earlier goals and objectives, as well as preliminary strategic thoughts. Figure 8.5 is the final result of Chapters One through Eight.
3. Strategies for your marketing plan are indicated on Figure 8.4; the goals that they help you attain are listed on Figure 8.5.

Chapter Nine:
The Marketing Plan

Now you can assemble your marketing plan.

Your overriding marketing objective is to find people to buy enough of your products and services, for enough money, and often enough to ensure a solid profit margin. Your marketing plan helps keep your business focused on the steps necessary to reach or exceed your goals.

Your marketing plan should not be long. If it becomes much longer than twenty pages, it won't be used. Individual elements that back it up may be lengthy, however. An advertising/promotional plan, for example, may run much longer. Sales plans for individual products, product lines, or services can become immensely detailed. (See Chapter Ten.)

The market plan must be succinct. It summarizes the analyses and strategies of the preceding eight chapters—so in one sense, you've already written it. Writing out your formal marketing plan gives you another chance to review your ideas and goals. If you haven't involved your staff in the planning process, this is a good time to get their ideas.

The key section of your marketing plan (Figure 9.2) is Section 7: How will you achieve these goals? You have four strategic variables to play with: Product/Service, Price, Location, and Promotion. Each of these can be subdivided further (see Figure 9.1) and tailored to meet the wants of your target markets.

There is no mechanical method of grinding out how to reach your goals. Your judgment and experience have to find expression here. The most common reason that strategies fail is that the fundamentals of implementing the game plan are done poorly or not at all. It doesn't matter how good your strategy is if it isn't properly executed.

The strategic variables must be considered in light of your present and prospective target markets. In fact, all your marketing plans should focus on meeting the needs and wants of these markets.

> **Your overriding marketing objective is to find people to buy enough of your products and services, for enough money, and often enough to ensure a solid profit margin.**

Figure 9.1
Aspects of the Four Strategic Marketing Variables

Make sure the aspects of each variable that pertain to your business complement one another.

Product/Service:
New, modified, new application
Position on life cycle
    Cash cow?
    Rising star?
    Dog?
    Owner's ego?
Benefits to purchaser
Perceived value

Price:
To end user
To distributors and to trade
    (What margins do you allow distributors and trade?)
Image
Market penetration
Markets' sensitivity to price changes

Place:
Location
Signs
Direct mail
Direct sales
Telemarketing

Promotion:
Advertising (including Yellow Pages, classified ads, and so on)
Public relations
Trade shows
Packaging
Special promotions (sales, spotlights, etc.)
Personal selling
Sales force training
Marketing support
Image: point of purchase, layout, lighting, stocking
Personal letters

Figure 9.2
Suggested Outline of Marketing Plan

1. Mission statement
   (What you want your business, main markets, and products/services to be.)
2. **Marketing objectives for next year and for the next three years**
   (These are the broad marketing objectives of Figure 1.5.)
3. **Sales and profit goals for next year and the next three years**
   (See Figure 1.5.)
4. Products/Services
   (Brief description by product/service lines, including proposed changes and any recent changes that would affect marketing goals. See Figure 2.3.)
5. Target markets
   (List and briefly describe. See Figure 2.4.)
6. Market potential
   (What size are the markets and what potential sales, profit, or other advantages does each have? See Figure 3.6.)
7. **How will you achieve your goals?**
   A. Overall strategy (See Figure 8.4.)
   B. Competitive strategies (See Figure 4.6.)
   C. Promotion strategies (See Figure 7.3.)
   D. Pricing, location, and sales practices (Brief statement of pricing strategy from Figure 5.3, plus brief statements about location, hours, and selling practices from Chapter Five if important or changed from normal patterns.)
   E. Marketing and advertising budgets
8. Potential problems
   (Brief description, plus proposed solutions, from Figure 8.1.)
9. **Implementation and measurement of timetables and benchmarks**
   (See Figure 10.2: Sales and Marketing Timetables.)
10. **Review and evaluation schedule**
    (Short schedule of important review dates.)

Appendix: Include supporting documents such as letters of intent, purchase agreements, and so forth if you think documentation is needed.

Chapter Ten:
The Sales Plan

The Marketing Plan defines the strategic directions for your business's marketing. The Sales Plan is the implementation tool for those grand strategies. Use Figure 10.1: Marketing Action Plan and Figure 10.2: Marketing Action Timetable to help organize actions and assign responsibility for their achievement. The goals come from your marketing plan (see Figures 8.2 and 8.5). The strategic boundaries (permissible methods, resources available, competitive considerations, and so on) are your responsibility—and must be considered in setting down the action steps.

Three major guidelines to keep in mind here are:

1. Establishing objective and measurable goals with deadlines. Broad, fuzzily defined sales goals are useless.

2. Assigning one person (yourself, perhaps) to oversee the action steps. Shared responsibility means nobody is responsible.

3. Discussing the action steps, timetables, and resources with the person responsible for attaining the objectives. If possible, involve everyone who works on the objective; this helps assure their cooperation. If your employees know clearly what you are trying to achieve, why it is important to attain that goal in time and within the resources allotted, and how progress will be measured, they will come up with ways to reach that goal.

There are six steps to the Marketing Action Plan:

1. State the goal.

2. Assign a target date for achieving the overall objective.

3. Assign responsibility to a single person.

4. Define the action steps. Achieving the objective requires that certain action steps be taken in a logical sequence. The more definitive the action steps, the better—since they can be more easily monitored.

5. For each action step, assign a target date. You may also want to assign responsibility for finishing the step to another person; delegation may be the only way to attain these mediate goals. Include the resources needed for each action step, and keep track of them. (Budgets are needed here—but that's another matter.)

6. Track the results, for progress and for future use.

The purpose of Figure 10.1 is to help you put together a tactical plan. Achieving the broad marketing objectives is like winning a war, while reaching these mediate goals is like winning individual battles. The tactics—the short-term activities which must be marshalled together to reach the strategic objectives—are highly detailed, but governed by the broad strategic guidelines established beforehand. Tactics only make sense in the context of strategy. Otherwise they are just random, undirected actions.

Tactics only make sense in the context of strategy.

Figure 10.1:
Marketing Action Plan

By: GL   Date: 2/27/87

Strategic Objective:

Action Steps	Target Date	Person Responsible	Results
1. Identify 100 prospects.	ASAP 3/87	GJB	
2. Call on prospects in reverse order of desirability – 3 each week.	9/87	GJB	
3. Make proposals to 10.	11/87	GJB	
4. Close 3	12/87	GJB	

You may wish to break this process down even further, and fill out one of these forms for each goal and each major action step involved. For example, if your goal is to increase net profits from Product A by $10,000 by the end of the next quarter, you might find that you have a considerable number of action steps to take: hiring and training a new salesperson; preparation of marketing support, advertising and promotional materials; setting a new guarantee; repackaging and repositioning the product; opening a new target market—all the while making sure that it doesn't affect other lines.

Once you have arrived at the action steps and their tentative due dates, timing becomes more and more important. One way to handle the timing problem is to work backward from the target dates. When do you have to start an action step? What steps along the way are critical to reaching the target dates? The more of these intermediate dates you can establish the better; they provide benchmarks to help keep the process of attaining the goals (and hence the strategic objectives) on schedule.

Use your judgment in choosing which steps to pin down to the tight scheduling of Figure 10.2 on the next page. You want to strike a balance between no controls and too much control.

Figure 10.2:
Marketing Action Timetable

By: _GL_ Date: _2/28/87_

Action Step: _Identify prospects_ Target Date: _4/87_

Completed: Not Completed but Due: _4/7/87_

List:

Sub-Steps	Completion Criteria (Benchmarks)	Dates of Completion
1. Yellow Pages	3/15/87	3/12/87
2. D & B	3/22/87	3/13/87
3. Drive around	4/1/87	4/7/87
4. Clip ads from local papers	ongoing	ongoing
5.		
6.		

Summary for Chapter Ten
1. Figures 10.1 and 10.2 provide an implementation and control system for your marketing plan.
2. If you assign product line (or service line) responsibility to an employee or colleague, work through these figures with him or her. The more people involved in setting the due dates and completion criteria the better—and their ideas on implementation can make a great contribution.
3. A Sales Plan is simply a compilation of Figures 10.1 and 10.2 for each product and/or service. Since you work out the detailed steps one by one with the overall Marketing Plan strategies in mind, reaching these more limited goals will help you attain the marketing objectives.
4. The reviews and evaluations help keep the plan on time and on target—and will help you improve your skills.
5. The Marketing Plan is a strategic plan, that is, it makes sure that you do the right things. The Sales Plan is tactical; it helps you do things right. You need both.

Appendices One and Two

Appendix One

Summary of Questions and Marketing Plan Outline

Part One: Summary of Major Questions in *The Market Planning Guide.*

Chapter One: Marketing Overview

Question 1: What business are you in?

Question 2: What do you sell?

Question 3: What are your target markets?

Question 4: What are your marketing goals for next year? Your sales and profit goals?

Question 5: What might keep you from achieving these goals?

Question 6: What is your marketing budget?

Chapter Two: Products and Services

Question 7: What are the benefits of your products/services?

Question 8: What is special about your products/services?

Question 9: What product/service is the best contributor to your overhead and profits (O & P)? What product/service is the biggest drain on your overhead and profits?

Chapter Three: Customers and Prospects

Question 10: Who are your current customers?

Question 11: What are their buying habits?

Question 12: Why do your customers buy your goods/services?

Question 13: Who are your best customers and prospects?

Question 14: What is your market share?

Question 14A: Is your market share growing, shrinking, or stable?

Question 14B: Is the market growing, shrinking, or stable? Is it changing in other ways?

Chapter Four: Competitive Analysis
Question 15: Who are your competitors?

Question 16: What do your competitors do better than you?

Question 17: What do you do better than your competitors?

Question 18: What is your competitive position?

Chapter Five: Price, Location, and Sales Practices
Question 19: How do you establish prices?

Question 20: How does your location affect you?

Question 21: What are your sales practices?

Chapter Six: Strengths and Weaknesses
Question 22: What is your business strong at?

Question 23: What is your business weak at?

Chapter Seven: Advertising and Promotion
Question 24: What is your advertising and promotion budget?

Question 25: What are your advertising and promotion objectives?

Question 26: How do you promote your business?

Chapter Eight: Strategic Marketing

Question 27: What marketing problems have you discovered so far?

Question 28: How do you plan to solve these problems?

Question 29: Are the goals stated in Chapter One still valid? If not, what are your new goals?

Question 30: How do you plan to achieve these goals?

Part Two: Outline of a Marketing Plan

1. **Mission statement**
   (What you want your business, main markets, and products/services to be.)
2. **Marketing objectives for next year and for the next three years**
   (These are the broad marketing objectives of Figure 1.5.)
3. **Sales and profit goals for next year and the next three years**
   (See Figure 1.5.)
4. **Products/Services**
   (Brief description by product/service lines, including proposed changes and any recent changes that would affect marketing goals. See Figure 2.3.)
5. **Target markets**
   (List and briefly describe. See Figure 2.4.)
6. **Market potential**
   (What size and potential sales, profit, or other advantages do these have? See Figure 3.6.)
7. **How will you achieve your goals?**
   A. Overall strategy (See Figure 8.4)
   B. Competitive strategies (See Figure 4.6.)
   C. Promotion strategies (See Figure 7.3.)
   D. Pricing, location, and sales practices (Brief statement of pricing strategy from Figure 5.3, plus brief statements about location, hours, and selling practices from Chapter Five if important or changed from normal patterns.)
   E. Marketing and advertising budgets
8. **Potential problems**
   (Brief description, plus proposed solutions, from Figure 8.1.)
9. **Implementation and measurement of timetables and benchmarks**
   (See Figure 10.2, Sales and Marketing Timetables.)
10. **Review and evaluation schedule**
    (Short schedule of important review dates)

Appendix: Include supporting documents such as letters of intent, purchase agreements, and so forth if you think documentation is needed.

Appendix Two

Bibliography and Resources

Bibliography

There are many excellent texts available on small business management, but most are more appropriate for businesses with more than 100 employees. Check out your local library, college bookstores, and these sources of small business management information:

1. **Upstart Publishing Company, Inc.:** *Profit Improvement Guides.* This series of handbooks on proven management techniques for small businesses is available from Upstart Publishing Company, Inc., 12 Portland Street, Dover, NH 03820. For ordering information and prices, call 800-235-8866 outside New Hampshire or 749-5071 in state.

   The series consists of the following books:

   The Business Planning Guide, © 1979, 1983, 1987, David H. Bangs, Jr. and Upstart Publishing Company, Inc. A 160-page manual that helps you write a business plan and financing proposal tailored to your business, your goals, and your resources. Includes worksheets and checklists.

   The Personnel Planning Guide, © 1988, David H. Bangs, Jr. and Upstart Publishing Company, Inc. A 160-page manual outlining practical and proven personnel management techniques, including hiring, managing, evaluating, and compensating personnel. Includes worksheets and checklists.

   The Cash Flow Control Guide, © 1988, David H. Bangs, Jr. and Upstart Publishing Company, Inc. A 75-page manual to help small business owners solve their number-one financial problem. Includes worksheets and checklists.

   The Market Planning Guide, © 1988, David H. Bangs, Jr. and Upstart Publishing Company, Inc. A 105-page manual to help small business owners put together a goal-oriented, resource-based marketing plan with action steps, benchmarks, and timelines. Includes worksheets and checklists to make implementation and review easier.

   How to Earn More Profits Through the People Who Work for You, William H. Scott, © 1982, Prentice-Hall. Currently out of print, but available from Bill Scott, c/o Upstart Publishing Co., Inc., 12 Portland Street, Dover, NH 03820. $7.95/copy, shipping & handling included.

   Profit Improvement Handbooks, Upstart Publishing Company, Inc. This is a series of booklets on all phases of managing a small business. Each handbook offers a concise, focused introduction aimed at a particular area of management. Topics range from strategic planning, to inventory management, to analyzing financial ratios, to planning a benefits program, to export marketing. Over sixty topics are available. These too can be imprinted with your logo and promotional information. These booklets have been used as collateral material, bank calling officer tools, and as part of successful direct mail programs. Contact the publisher for a complete list of topics.

2. ***Small Business Reporter***. An excellent series of booklets on small business management published by Bank of America, Department 3120, PO Box 37000, San Francisco, CA 94137. 1-415-622-2491. Individual copies are $5 each. Ask for a list of current titles—they have about 17 available, including *Steps to Starting a Business, Avoiding Management Pitfalls, Business Financing,* and *Marketing Small Business.*

3. ***In Business***. A bimonthly magazine for small businesses, especially those with fewer than 10 employees. The publisher is J.G. Press, PO Box 323, Emmaus, PA 18049. Annual subscriptions are $18.

4. ***The Great Brain Robbery***, Ray Considine and Murray Raphel, © 1980, 1981, by The Great Brain Robbery, 1360 East Rubio Street, Altadena, CA 91101. Subtitled "A collection of proven ideas to make you money and change your life!," *The Great Brain Robbery* contains numerous checklists and ideas which are thought-provoking. The chapters entitled "Formula for Success," "Secret Selling Sentences," and "If You Don't Like It Here, Get Out!" are particularly provocative. Raphel and Considine are marketing and promotional experts—which is apparent throughout this book.

5. ***Marketing with Facts***, © 1986, published by Price Waterhouse, 1251 Avenue of the Americas, New York, NY 10020. This book, part of a series aimed at small business owners and entrepreneurs, focuses on how marketing information can be used to enhance opportunities for profit. The book's lists of questions and lexicon of marketing terminology are particularly helpful. Copies of this book cost $5.00 and are available at any Price Waterhouse office.

Other Tools for Small Business Owners

Upstart Video. We have a videotape based on *The Business Planning Guide.* Call 800-235-8866 outside New Hampshire and 749-5071 in-state for more information.

Software for small businesses. The best integrated planning package for small business owners we've come across is Plans 'n Totals™, which requires an IBM PC or equivalent with 512K RAM. Plans 'n Totals™ provides menus to help prepare financial projections and budgets, and then helps you analyze them (break-even and ratio analysis are built in). Call 617-264-4450, or write to Resource N Corporation, 66 Commonwealth Avenue, Concord, MA 01742 for current price information. A demo disk is available.

Our favorite spreadsheets are Excel™ and Multiplan™ for the Macintosh, and Lotus 1-2-3™ for the IBM PC and compatibles. You may find ready-made templates for specific business applications available from local computer clubs.

Resources

1. **Small Business Development Centers** (SBDCs). Call your state university or the Small Business Administration (SBA) to find the SBDC nearest to you. One of the best free management programs available, SBDCs provide expert assistance and training in every aspect of business management. Don't ignore this resource.

2. **SCORE**, or Service Corps of Retired Executives, sponsored by the U.S. Small Business Administration, provides free counseling and also a series of workshops and seminars for small businesses. Of special interest: SCORE offers a Business Planning Workshop which includes a 30-minute video produced specifically for SCORE by Upstart Publishing and funded by Paychex, Inc. There are over 500 SCORE chapters nationwide. For more information contact the SBA office nearest you and ask about SCORE.

3. **Small Business Administration** (SBA). Besides the numerous lending programs, the SBA has a number of management assistance programs. These programs are subject to frequent change due to Congressional mandates and budgetary requirements. The SBA also co-sponsors many workshops and seminars and has an extensive library of small business literature. The SBA is listed in the white pages of your phone book under "U.S. Government."

4. **Colleges and universities**. Most have business courses. Some have SBDCs, others have more specialized programs. Some have small business expertise—the University of New Hampshire, for example, has two schools which provide direct small business management assistance.

5. **Keye Productivity Center**, PO Box 23192, Kansas City, MO 64141. Keye Productivity offers business seminars on specific personnel topics for a reasonable fee. Call them at 800-821-3919 for topics and prices. Their seminar entitled "Hiring and Firing" is excellent, well-documented, and useful. Good handout materials are included.

6. **Comprehensive Accounting Corporation**, 2111 Comprehensive Drive, Aurora, IL 60507. CAC has over 425 franchised offices providing accounting, bookkeeping, and management consulting services to small businesses. For information, call 800-323-9009.

7. **Center for Entrepreneurial Management**, 180 Varick Street, 17th Floor, New York, NY 10014. The oldest and largest nonprofit membership association for small business owners in the world. They maintain an extensive list of books, videotapes, cassettes, and other small business management aids. Call 212-633-0060 for information.

8. **Libraries.** Do not forget to take advantage of the information readily available at your library.